The Power of Allegiances

IDENTITY, CULTURE, AND REPRESENTATIONAL STRATEGIES

Essay Series 33

Marino Tuzi

The Power of Allegiances

IDENTITY, CULTURE, AND
REPRESENTATIONAL STRATEGIES

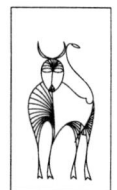

Guernica
Toronto/Buffalo/Lancaster
1997

Copyright © 1997 by Marino Tuzi and Guernica Editions Inc.
All rights reserved. The use of any part of this publication, reproduced,
transmitted in any form or by any means, electronic, mechanical,
photocopying, recording or otherwise stored in a retrieval system, without
the prior consent of the publisher is an infringement of the copyright law.
Typeset by Selina.

Antonio D'Alfonso, Editor
Guernica Editions Inc.
P.O. Box 117, Station P, Toronto (ON), Canada M5S 2S6
250 Sonwil Drive, Buffalo, N.Y. 14225-5516 U.S.A.
Gazelle, Falcon House, Queen Square, Lancaster LA1 1RN U.K.

The publication of this book was made possible thanks to grants received
from The Canada Council, The Ontario Arts Council,
and The Department of Canadian Heritage.

Legal Deposit — Third Quarter
National Library of Canada
Library of Congress Catalog Card Number: 96-79288

Canadian Cataloguing in Publication Data
Marino, Tuzi, 1952-
The power of allegiances : identity, culture,
and representational strategies
(Essay series ; no. 33)
ISBN 1-55071-029-X
1. Canadian fiction (English) — Minority authors —
History and criticism.
2. Canadian fiction (English) — 20th century —
History and criticism.
3. Identity in literature.
I. Titles. II. Series: Essay series (Toronto, Ont.) ; no. 33.
PS8199.T89 1997   C813'.5409'8   C96-900876-7
PR9192.5T89   1997

Contents

1. Writing the Minority Subject 7
2. Provisionality, Multiplicity, and the Ironies of Identity
   in *Black Madonna* 33
3. Indeterminancy, Border States of Consciousness,
   and *Other Selves* 58
4. Disjunction and Paradox: *Lives of the Saints* and
   The Deromanticization of the Old World 74
5. Discontinuity and Femininity: *Made in Italy*'s
   Contestation of Italian Patriarchy 100
6. The Social Construction of Subjectivity
   in *The Lion's Mouth*. 121
7. Fairy Tales and *Bottled Roses*:
   Deconstructing the Stereotypes 142
8. Conclusion: Form, Identity, and Present
   and Future Trajectories 156
9. Theoretical Afterword: Minority Writing, Culture,
   Agency, and Representation 168
10. Notes 184
11. List of Works Cited 193

Acknowledgements

The advice that I received from John Lennox was invaluable in the shaping of the form and direction of this book. I also benefited from my fruitful exchanges with Susan Warwick and Gordon Darroch. I am grateful to Clara Thomas who encouraged me to undertake an analysis of this area of literary activity. Joseph Pivato provided worthwhile suggestions when I revised the material for publication. Equally important was Antonio D'Alfonso's counsel and patience when I was in the process of preparing the manuscript for Guernica Editions.

I want to recognize members of my family for their ongoing support: my parents, Pietro Tuzi and Domenica Facchini Tuzi; my sisters, Antonette Tuzi Stirling, Marisa Tuzi, and Tina Tuzi; and my brothers-in-law, Jim Stirling and Jacques Siegrist. Lastly, I wish to express my gratitude to Marianne Coulon, my life companion, with whom I shared many moments of challenge and illumination.

I dedicate this study to those writers who have worked assiduously in helping to create a unique body of literature and criticism.

1
Writing the Minority Subject

Fictional texts by Italian Canadian writers enter the discourse on ethnicity by exploring the dilemmas of identity formation in a complex cultural topography. In these texts, the subject usually is situated precariously at the interstice of a new and evolving, urban-centred social order and an agrarian-based, albeit altered ethnic community. Italian Canadian identity is shaped by a given social context and is not represented as a unitary concept or cohesive reality. Beset by an array of adverse and often irreconcilable viewpoints, the ethnic protagonist fashions a self-image in relation to several competing belief systems.

The dramatization of the ethnic condition involves a persistent maneuvering among partial and incongruous cultural perspectives. The ethnic subject must constantly rethink his/her social positioning. The volatilility of Italian Canadianness is manifested in states of anxiety, estrangement, and irresolution.

Such provisionality is compounded by the internal instability of both mainstream and Italian culture, since each cultural context is itself heterogenous and mutable and, therefore, not reducible to a discrete assortment of traits, values, and beliefs. The many connections between the two cultures are tentative because the Italian Canadian subject continues to reposition himself/herself in a dynamic and pluralistic urban environment. There is a reluctance to commit oneself to values and assumptions that may circumscribe the various social contexts and which, ironically, provide a basis for self-definition.

Cultural dissonance, the presence of contradictory and transitory social stimuli, and the experience of alienation are manifested in the Italian Canadian text in the form of a fragmented, multilayered, and largely undefinable ethnic identity. Attitudes associated with the social, class, and gender position of the protagonist in the minority group and in the mainstream community become part of the enactment of ethnic subjectivity. These positionings, as ways of making sense of the world, are brought into the text's characterization of the Italian Canadian subject. Men and women are depicted as being formed by diverse cultural contexts which provide the "raw material" for self-development. The interactions between the Italian community and English Canadian society imply that sometimes it is possible for the protagonist to negotiate some kind of provisional cultural identity; however, there often is no final resolution, because the content, shape, and direction of this new identity are mutable.

1. *Social Context*

The social text embedded in the works of Italian Canadian writers sets critical reference points for the discourse on identity formation. Etymologically, the Greek word *ethnos* means nation or people. It also describes a people who share the same language and culture. In Canada, the term ethnic is commonly used to allude to a person whose cultural background is neither English nor French. This person is deemed to belong to a minority group. The use of the term *minority* is not based solely on such features as culture, language, race, and religion, but also on the fact that an ethnic group is smaller in number and usually occupies the lower levels of the socioeconomic structure: "Ethnicity . . . represents the sum total of attributes and practices of an ethnocultural group . . . [but it is also] related to the social meaning assigned to the items on the list. The social meaning usually includes minority status and the experience of subordination, a subordination based along ethnic lines."[1] Ethnicity is a deeply politicized phenomenon because "it is a particular system of acting/displaying being ethnic"[2] that is a consequence of socioeconomic inequality. Linda Hutcheon believes that "the word 'ethnic' always has to do with the social positioning of the 'other,' and is thus never free of relations of power and value."[3]

A member of an ethnic community confronts a new social context, in which cultural assumptions, standards of conduct, and value systems contest the legitimacy of tradition and accepted forms of behaviour. The organization of human activity in the host country produces a series of dislocations and transformations in the work and modes of living of the individual. Peter Li claims that "the present conditions" of industrial capitalism in Canada have been responsible for "determining how ethnicity is expressed."[4] Admittedly, Li is elaborating on an idea about ethnicity that is shared by several American sociologists: Yancey, Ericksen, and Juliani posit that "the development and persistence of ethnicity is dependent upon structural conditions characterizing American cities and the position of groups in American social structure."[5] Likewise, John Edwards theorizes that the persistence of ethnicity is attributable to the adaptability of minority groups whose "distinctive cultures" are to a large extent "creations growing out of their experiences on American soil."[6] Li and his American counterparts concur that ethnicity is changed by social and economic circumstances. In their discussion of ethnic subjectivity, Abdul R. JanMohamed and David Lloyd note that " 'becoming minor' is not a question of essence (as the stereotypes of minorities in dominant ideology would want us to believe) but a question of position: a subject position that in the final analysis can be defined only in 'political' terms — that is, in terms of the effects of economic exploitation, political disenfranchisement, social manipulation, and ideological domination on the cultural formation of minority subjects and discourses."[7] This reading of ethnicity in the United States is relevant to the study of minority experience in Canada.

Since ethnicity is motivated by social and economic factors, the identity of the minority person is not homogenous or singular. Given that "ethnicity is [a] continuous variable,"[8] similar conditions will affect individual members of an ethnic group, such as parents and relatives, in different ways. For instance, Frank Paci observes that second generation Italian Canadians often react to the pressures of assimilation by absorbing the dominant language and world view. If Italian Canadians discard their mother tongue and tradition, it is because they see their parents and their customs "as foreign to their Canadian sensibility."[9]

Radical discontinuity between parents and children is one index of how the host country may alter the life of the newcomer. Socioeconomic structures of the mainstream society and the attendant pull towards acculturation also can reshape the identities of parents and their children. In turn, the process of adjustment results in the creation of a variegated group identity.[10] Minority members participate in "diverse modes of identity" and "these multiple identities are neither reducible nor impermeable to one another."[11] Reality, for the ethnic subject, is composed of a host of "temporalities and histories."[12] Reality involves the intertwining of many cultural elements found both in the minority group and the dominant society. Not only is ethnic identity manifold, it is also unfixed, interminably modified by evolving and dissimilar social contexts. This unfolding[13] underlines the multi-facetedness and indeterminacy of the ethnic subject.

Social and historical scholars of Italians in Canada advance the idea that the culture of the newcomer is reconstituted in the host society. Admitting that the ethnicity of the immigrant began "in the home town," John Zucchi maintains that "certain conditions in Toronto . . . [led to a] heightened ethnic consciousness."[14] Robert Harney points to "the hybrid result of a Toronto ethnogenesis in the late 1960s and the 1970s"[15] which was marked by "variations in emblems of identity over time."[16] Likewise, Giuliana Colalillo describes the formation of "a syncretic [ethnic] culture"[17] in which immigrant family members combined old and new cultural elements at home and work.

In the postwar period, the building of a modern infrastructure in Montreal and Toronto required "the delicate melding of paesanism and occupational skill" on the part of Italians.[18] These immigrants were employed in the construction of the urban infrastructure (such as sewers, roads, subways) and buildings (such as homes, factories, and office towers). The blending of "a pre-industrial peasant past with an industrial urban present" produced an identity that was multiple; it was "neither an Italian nor a Canadian entity, but rather an 'Italo-Canadian' one."[19]

Roberto Perin, however, is reluctant to accept the notion of a cultural synthesis, since it remains unclear to him whether the new identity of the Italian replaced or co-existed with the original.[20] Nevertheless, he suggests that a kind of transformation took place because "the immigrant's culture could not, any more than some hypothetical Italian culture, survive intact in North America."[21] The newcomer brought "a particularistic ancient Mediterranean culture" which was modified "in response to [the] North American environment."[22] Noting that "context" tends "to alter the form and meaning of behaviour," Perin asserts that "it would be more appropriate, if we were to retain biological images, to speak of mutation."[23]

The resilience of Italian immigrants was rooted in the old country; family members consolidated their labour and resources in response to the harsh realities of rural life. Leo Cellini surmises that the extended family was not "an end in itself," since it embodied an "adaptive characteristic" of "developing communities" coping with urbanization, modernization, and over-population.[24] By force of circumstance, the family structure in Southern Italy was not static and homogeneous, but "dynamic and heterogeneous."[25] There were certain features that characterized family relations. Edward Banfield states that in Southern Italy during the 1950s an adult individual scarcely had a sense of self that was distinct from the identity of the family.[26] The intensity of kin relations, observes Clifford Jansen, usually minimized the importance of "any larger national, regional or even local community."[27] According to Franc Sturino, the nuclear and extended family claimed the individual member's allegiance and bound him/her to a set of reciprocal rights and obligations.[28] The valorization of family did not erase individualism or make loyalty to and identification with the family unconditional. Individualism took shape through one's rank in the family and this was often based on a person's economic contribution. Devotion to the family at times depended on its ability to meet the person's needs.

Immigration to Canada and the need to establish a common strategy in an unfamiliar socioeconomic context led to subtle shifts in the roles played by members of the family. While the father controlled the behaviour of his wife and children,[29] the practicality of having his wife maintain the household while he worked reduced his authority. The woman "enjoyed a higher status than could be expected in a supposedly patriarchal society such as the Italian south," and her "compliance was more in the nature of carrying out patterns of behaviour than in an imbued or inculcated sense of submission."[30] She was indispensable to the domestic and social organization of the family[31] because she kept house, cared for the children, and ensured that the husband's earnings were prudently used. In deploying the domestic skills that were learned in the old country, the Italian woman extended the family's food and clothing resources through vegetable gardens and sewing.[32] The crucial functions of the woman as wife and mother were indicative of a family structure that was at once patrilineal and matrifocal.[33]

According to Franca Iacovetta, the woman's transition from "*contadina* [peasant] to worker did not require a fundamental break" from traditional patriarchal values[34]: she had long been accustomed to arduous labour in the household. It required a certain reorientation of her role in the family. When the woman became a worker, her relation to her husband changed because she no longer toiled solely in the home. While her income was supplementary to the man's, it "replenished the male bread-winner and fed, clothed and raised children."[35] Consequently, she attained both a different kind of economic importance and a relative autonomy that challenged the man's traditional socioeconomic centrality in the household. The combined efforts of the woman and her husband made it possible to save money to purchase a house. Although a common struggle to build a new life in the host country necessitated a form of cooperation, this socioeconomic collaboration did not eradicate the conflictual power relations between husband and wife.

The social and institutional environment of the children — primarily in terms of the school system, the media, and the impinging English Canadian mainstream culture — helped to form their view of the world. This view was frequently in conflict with the traditional values of their parents. At the same time, the children continued to retain components of their immigrant culture in their family and community life. Inevitably, these components began to intersect with aspects of their Canadian identity.

Members of the second generation also found themselves at variance with the Canadian mainstream. Feeling the push and pull of two distinct cultures — even though the culture of the parents had been altered by their experience in the host country — second generation Italians (and most of the writers to be discussed belong to this group) who were socialized in the late 1960s and in the early 1970s rearranged their value system to contend with competing social systems.

The cultural gap between the two generations "proved to be a severe test for the strategy of acculturation of many Italian families."[36] Italian immigrant parents wanted their children to follow traditional family values, but, as the children assimilated into the mainstream, these values were either modified or discarded.[37] North American society promulgated an individualism that made corporate family values such as filial obedience, marriage, and patriarchal gender roles, if not painfully irrelevant, then at least secondary to the adult children's desire for personal actualization. Although the parents advocated educational and professional advancement as a strategy for their children's economic achievement, social mobility often threatened the fabric of traditional family life. Many children chose to live on their own in early adulthood. Some daughters rejected patriarchal-matrifocal notions of femininity and aspired to a professional career.[38]

If the Italian family in general "proved capable of absorbing the shocks of intergenerational conflict,"[39] it was because a form of accommodation was achieved. Often this accommodation was built into the structure of the family itself. Since the family was "corporate in its nature, owning property in common," the "main function of this common wealth was to enable the parents successfully to *sistemare* their children at the time of marriage, that is to say, to set them up as independent adults, ideally in their own household."[40] Parents also aided their children by funding their post-secondary education.[41] The project of *sistemazione,* which stressed family and economic security, constructed the base for the children's success as adults. Parental support was not given without implied obligations on the children, such as caring for the parents in their old age, offering continual hospitality to them in their homes, or providing ongoing assistance so that parents could deal with their medical, legal, and financial matters.

Italianness, as a marker of the cultural distinctiveness of the first and second generation, is associated with a series of qualities which derive from the social practices and expressed beliefs of an historically-specific immigrant community. Italianness in Canada is a reworking of established assumptions and habits, and is even a reinvention of particular modes of behaviour. Italianness is composed of an assortment of converging, sometimes opposed, and ever-mutable cultural traits. Even in the old country, the social relations which influenced Italian identity — such as the extended family, with its gender-defined roles — were conflictual and in a state of flux. Italianness in the old and new world is a fluid social construct, and not a compendium of natural and timeless attributes, so it is true that the Canadianness of the ethnic subject is an aggregate of diverse social components which are malleable and frequently inconsistent.

2. *Textual Production*

The social ground of the Italian Canadian experience involves a process of transformation and contradiction. William Boelhower contends that, in minority writing, ethnicity in the host country "seems to generate the language of identity in the form of an endless production of questions."[42] The questioning of dominant and ethnic group beliefs thwarts the development of a unitary ethnic identity: "the ethnic sign is not socially fixed or predictable because its very position within the culture of the national map makes it peremptorily unstable."[43] Overtaken by such indeterminacy, the ethnic subject participates in a continual process of resignification: "the ethnic subject must inevitably define ethnicity as a means and not an end ... in the place of the real world [of the original culture] there is now only a global strategy of possible worlds."[44]

Achievement of a stable sense of self remains a hypothetical enterprise, since the Italian Canadian is constantly choosing from and being shaped by an array of infinite and changeable subject positions. What is constituted as an identity is prone to dissolution.

The ethnic subject's interpretation of the relationship of the two cultural systems — which are alternately approachable, intangible, and remote — is based on the contingencies of the moment. The ethnic subject constructs a self-image in order to cope with the disorienting effects of cultural multiplicity. William Boelhower argues that "as a pluralized and multiform self, the ethnic's very instability as well as his access to an open series of possible worlds make him unpredictable and aleatory. . . Because he [/she] is both inside and outside the dominant culture, his [/her] ethnic framing activity often becomes what surely must seem a contradictory strategy for producing ethnic discontinuity out of the very cultural continuum of the national map."[45] The incompatibility of perspectives results in social discontinuity and makes evident the relativity and internal disjunctions of each cultural context.

What remains constant is that ethnicity, in reaction to the assimilative pressures of the new society, reforms itself without severing its ties to cultural history and genealogy. Ethnicity is always there in the life of the protagonist, however displaced, incongruent, and indeterminate it is. The salience of ethnicity in mainstream society is characterized by what Sneja Gunew refers to as "an insistence on the untranslatability or incommensurability of cultural difference."[46]

Italian Canadian writing does not just address marginalization or cultural disjunction. Such a reading of ethnic literature is limiting. Ethnicity is perpetually unfolding, and it encompasses numerous discrepant and frequently overlaying cultural perspectives. Myrna Kostash notes that ethnicity abounds in contradiction and avoids any kind of fixity: "For my generation, however, the question has been posed again, and it has been posed not as a polarized conflict between the either/or assimilation and ghettoization but as the postmodern realization that we ethnic *arrivistes* live in both conditions at once. The point, suddenly, is not [Gabrielle] Roy's dream of the reconciliation of opposites but the acceptance, even cultivation, of what [Eli] Mandel has called the 'interface' of cultures . . . where tension at the point of contact, ambivalence, ambiguity, porousness, is the point, not resolution — the transcendence of paradox, stasis — as has been implied in the older dream."[47] The reorganization of identities and the criss-crossing of dissimilar cultural signifiers announce a "process of becoming"[48] in which a consolidation of perspective is perennially forestalled.

According to Frank Paci, the development of a new consciousness can be uncertain because it issues out of a "dialectic of historical change."[49] Antonio D'Alfonso promotes a view of ethnicity which speaks of continuous effort and multiplicity: "Struggle is the force behind the process of identity which manifests itself in different ways."[50] Citing the poetry of Filippo Salvatore, D'Alfonso observes a "never-ending search between the natural and the cultural, the Old and New World, between the past and present."[51] Italian Canadianness is many-sided because it interlocks various perspectives in the host country, and because the place of origin is itself composed of various regions and localities which resist cultural homogenization: "Italy is not a unity but a mosaic. Italians are seen not as a group but as individuals with distinct identities."[52]

For William Boelhower, ethnic writing is founded on the idea that identity is engaged in a constant play of subject-positions: "Given the copresence of cultural models and the principle of reversibility deriving from it, the ethnic subject is able to carry out his/her jeu of ambivalence, [to] break out of the unidirectionality of official cultural discourse. . . Such a practice of ethnic interrogation as this, and one finds it operating throughout the collection of *Roman Candles,* refuses to reduce the order of discourse to a single meaning, a single code or cultural model, and prefers instead a strategy of perspectival ambiguity."[53]

Meaning in an ethnic text is arranged in terms of "a topological system that generates an open series of such binary categories as Old World/New World; . . . origin/traces; continuity/discontinuity."[54] These binaries are not static; they are not always clearly defined, and they tend to collapse interminably, since the shifting ground of ethnicity undermines any fixed categorization of experience. In the ethnic text, the emergence of cultural binaries heralds the disjunctions, pluralities, and mutability of the Italian Canadian subject who persistently "floats between two worlds, two cultural models."[55]

This indefiniteness connotes the otherness of the ethnic subject, associated with dislocation, marginality, and difference, in a society where ethnicity is submerged because it lacks immediate cultural referents. The unavailability of accessible signs and codes to reconstruct a new identity paradoxically permits the acting out of endless possibilities and the cultivation of ambiguity.

Italian Canadian writing focuses as much on the perplexities and evolution of ethnicity as it does on the conflict between two disparate world views. The Italian Canadian text is steeped in "the endless uncertainties and ambiguities implied by the need . . . to create a self" and it revels in "the duplicities of self-creation, [of] the transformation of identities."[56] Italian Canadian literature shows how the ethnic subject is presented consistently with an assortment of cultural options which grow out of the experience of living simultaneously in two cultures.

3. *Italian Canadian Women Writers: Gender and Identity*

In the work of Italian Canadian women writers to be examined in this study (Maria Ardizzi, Caterina Edwards, and Darlene Madott), gender is at the core of the discourse on the ethnic subject's multiplicity. Although gender is not the main focus of their narratives, Frank Paci in *Black Madonna* and Nino Ricci in *Lives of the Saints* investigate gender relations in the new and old world in their delineation of Italian Canadian identity. The difference in emphasis between male and female writers indicates that there is a correlation between the fictional construction of gender and the way that gender is socially and culturally constituted. Italian Canadian women's writing invokes not just a femininized awareness of gender identity, but also the social text which historically has enclosed the life of the female subject.

The Italian Canadian woman's experience in the Italian family and Canadian society has been one of friction and disjunction. This situation is manifested in various forms in Maria Ardizzi's *Made in Italy*, Caterina Edwards' *The Lion's Mouth*, and Darlene Madott's *Bottled Roses*. In *Made in Italy*, the female protagonist fashions a gender identity from two patriarchal frameworks — Italian and Canadian — which are in themselves inconsistent and precarious. Interaction with mainstream society, primarily through work, provides her with a degree of financial and social autonomy which frustrates her husband's attempts to regulate her behaviour. The moment of emancipation is countered by her socioeconomic disenfranchisement in the host country as a woman and as an ethnic person. Inequality strengthens the bond with her family and reaffirms traditional attitudes about the woman's role in the immigrant community. Intergenerational discord, resulting from her children's assumption of mainstream values, subverts her role in the home. In *The Lion's Mouth* and *Bottled Roses*, this ambivalence is manifested, respectively, by second and third generation protagonists who have a deeper connection to the mainstream. Commitment to one cultural position is not possible without limiting available options and without denying critical parts of a multiple gender/ethnic identity. The female subject inhabits, is distanced from, and is suspended between contentious and intertwining cultural contexts.

The Italian community and Canadian society provide various models of femininity which reinforce or undermine each other: the common valorizing of being a wife and motherhood, and urban society's promotion of social and economic independence to the detriment of a group identity.

Feminine Italian Canadian identity is many-sided and disjunctive since it is affected by different social and cultural variables. Italian Canadian femininity is socially produced and continually revising itself in unstable circumstances. On the level of fictional representation, Italian Canadian women writers, as is the case with their American counterparts (according to Mary Jo Bona) "have recreated their ethnicity to accommodate the changing needs of women."[57]

Italian Canadian texts by women and men also suggest that traditional Italian masculinity is devalued in an urban-technological environment where the man experiences a loss of status. Likewise, the male must to some degree share power with his female counterpart in order to anchor himself in the host country. Despite this, the male maintains a privileged position in the household, while the patriarchal mindset of the dominant culture reinforces his masculine identity.

Like fictional texts which focus on the male protagonist, the narrative of the Italian Canadian woman, nevertheless, is characterized by a conflict of allegiances and points to a multiple gender/ethnic identity. Helen Barolini's view of Italian American women's writing is equally applicable to this study. She asserts that this kind of feminine narrative "exposes the signs and symbols, the auguries and directions of lives which were — and are — subject to great ambivalence, to . . . opposing cultural influence."[58]

4. *Formal Strategies and Themes*

A. Irony

The multiplicity, ambiguity and open-endedness of identity formation is represented in Italian Canadian fiction through a variety of formal strategies. These strategies destabilize the possibility of affixing a particular meaning to the events and actions depicted in the texts. Chief among these strategies is the use of irony which cultivates difference and contradiction, provides us with numerous views of a particular situation, and facilitates the exploration of ethnic identity. According to Linda Hutcheon, "irony is one of the discursive strategies used by . . . marginalized or 'minoritarian artists.' "[59]

By its very nature, irony is inclusive, not only allowing, but also delighting in the play of opposites. In the literary texts to be examined, the representation of the given protagonist's quest for a stable and singular identity is continually ironized, exposing not only the contradictory and conflicting elements that compose his/her identity, but also the provisionality of ethnicity: "irony is at least potential in not only anything doubled but anything problematic and relative."[60]

The ironies of ethnic identity also resolve themselves into an overriding paradox: ethnic subjects can only reconstitute a sense of self by coming to grips with their cultural multiplicity. Irony, then, is at the centre of what Boelhower calls the perspectival ambiguity of ethnic literature: "the transformative and destabilizing powers of irony" generate an inexhaustible host of meanings.[61]

B. Elegy

In the texts of Italian Canadian writers, the use of irony at times combines with the elegiac mode. The invocation of the homeland is tinged with regret and sorrow. Canadianization is marked by various degrees of cultural loss in tandem with a constant and often difficult process of behavioural modification. Counterbalancing this anxiety is the reenvisioning of bygone days as edenic moments in the life of the protagonist. Nostalgia for the old world, often expressed in tableau-like images of the physical and natural setting and of people left behind, is a compensatory gesture for the scarcity of familiar signposts in the Canadian mainstream. The social disorientation which accompanies immigration propels the protagonist to romanticize the lifestyle of the past. This idealization serves as a defense against the sometimes debilitating psychological and cultural effects of adjusting to the new country. The experience of displacement may also push back into the recesses of memory dark images of past adversity in the homeland. While producing a sense of cultural marginality, this dislocation tends to subsume an awareness of the historical cleavages and incongruities imbedded in Italian society. Social displacement intensifies the confusion felt by the protagonist in having to rework, because of the force of circumstance, the fabric of his/her cultural identity.

In Italian Canadian writing, the death of the first generation becomes a recurrent metaphor for cultural deracination and the attendant disappearance of certain established patterns of behaviour. Death also adumbrates the fear and anxiety of having to reinvent one's cultural identity in an unfamiliar and often oppressive socioeconomic environment. The lament for the passage of an "idyllic childhood"[62] is evident, for instance, in Minni's and Ricci's fictional works, and is ultimately paradoxical. The ethnic subject points to the experience of deterritorialization, of losing an identifiable frame of reference, while at the same time acknowledging that Italianness can only persist by incorporating elements of English Canadian culture.

The use of elegy further implies an underlying disillusionment about Italy. The old country is incapable of providing sustenance for its inhabitants. The elegiac mode serves to call into question the relevance of mainstream values since, despite its economic opportunities, Canada will not permit the recreation of established cultural patterns. The multi-textured tonality of Italian Canadian writing, with its blend of mournfulness, sentimentality, disillusionment, and scepticism, indicates the complex use that is made of the elegiac mode. Elegy highlights the contradictory and indeterminate cultural positioning of the ethnic subject; he/she "is the lost son [or daughter] of his [/her] home village" and appears to "not fully exist in the new society."[63]

C. Juxtaposition

Irony and elegy tend to rely on the contrast between two distinct and divergent cultures. As such, the use of contrast, a recurrent technique in Italian Canadian writing, keeps constantly before us a given text's many frames of reference as the texts shift back and forth between Italian and Canadian culture. Juxtaposition of diverse figurations, such as images, symbols and metaphors, is loaded with cultural meaning.

For William Boelhower, minority writing "suggests an aesthetics of spatial [and cultural] juxtaposition," and presents a "stereoscopic" perspective on ethnicity.[64] Juxtaposition frequently intimates a collision of world views, and serves to emphasize the fact that Italian Canadian identity is constructed out of a set of conflicting cultural positions. By placing other specific images and cultural referents next to each other — images and referents that are ideologically opposed — juxtaposition thematizes in different ways the dilemma of renegotiating a new ethnic identity: "The tension between wanting to belong to the new society and yet wanting to retain the culture of the old obviously varies from person to person in intensity and emotional weight."[65] Juxtaposition further involves the opposition of images within a specific cultural context, whether Italian or Canadian, and conveys the confusion of the ethnic subject's identity. Reality in either world is provisional; models of behaviour are continually revealed to be inconsistent and prone to dissolution in the face of shifting social and economic circumstances. By implying that coherence and stability are problematic in the old and the new, juxtaposition breaks down a simple division of viewpoints. Juxtaposition avoids binarism; it includes the convergence of commonly-held cultural positions. For instance, the juxtaposing of culturally-specific images associated with gender roles shows that certain segments of the Italian community and Canadian society are more inclined to valorize patriarchal notions of femininity and masculinity.

Through a series of juxtaposed but related scenes, the minority literary text demonstrates the compatibility between the immigrant project and the world of work. The members of the Italian Canadian family strategically deploy their combined labour and assets to achieve financial success. This thematic motif legitimates social mobility as one of the most prominent ideologies of contemporary capitalism. Thomas Ferraro's comment on the representation of ethnicity in American literature, which is relevant to this study, supports the idea that minority groups cooperate with the existing economic system: "European family structures and traditions do not necessarily dissolve in the face of capitalism but rather, as they have always done, evolve to meet its changing needs."[66]

In its own way, the ethnic text reinscribes some of the prevailing ideological premises of mainstream capitalist society. At the same time, it contests other ideas, such as materialism and individualism, which threaten the viability of family-centred social relations. The ironic juxtaposition of the lives of Canadianized adult children to those of their immigrant parents dramatizes the encounter of ethnic and North American cultural ideologies. Second generation characters, such as Marie Barone in *Black Madonna* and Andrea Moratti in *Made in Italy*, often valorize middle-classness because of its apparently higher level of refinement, social privileges, and affluence. These characters appear to dismiss the working-class ethnic lifestyle of their parents which is perceived to be culturally regressive and dependent for its survival on menial labour.

The bourgeois orientation of the assimilated protagonists separates them from their traditionally-minded parents, but this class positioning is not completely at variance with the immigrant project in Canada. The first generation, as represented by such characters as Assunta and Adamo Barone in *Black Madonna* and Nora and Giovanni Moratti in *Made in Italy*, made use of their particular skills at home and in the workplace and shared their economic resources, adhering to the norms of the Southern Italian family. They did so in order to improve their immediate social and economic standing in Canada, and to ensure a stable and prosperous future for their children.

Juxtaposition as an "investigative technique"[67] unravels the paradoxes of ethnicity in a complex and changeable social terrain. By relentlessly examining distinct cultural contexts and their contrast to other cultures, Italian Canadian writing illuminates the density and capriciousness of ethnic identity. In general, according to Linda Hutcheon, ethnic literary texts exhibit an unfaltering "capacity for ambiguity, juxtaposition, and irony."[68]

D. Imagery

Italian Canadian literature makes symbolic use of images which capture unique elements of immigrant culture and mainstream society. Such symbolism and imagery underline the ironic, elegiac, and manifold representation of ethnicity. Image patterns associated with tradition-bound peasant culture generate contradictory significations. For example, the recurrence of the garden image, part of the first generation's attempt to reconstruct their agrarian surroundings in the new world, is a culturally charged motif, the symbolic meanings of which produce an ambivalent view of the immigrant experience. The garden is simultaneously a testament to the persistence of the old way of life and the celebration of one of the most important accomplishments of the Italian Canadian: the acquisition of a home. Yet the cultivation of a small garden in the backyard implies that the former immigrant has undergone a process of diminution; he/she has given up the open fields of the family farm for a little patch of land in the new country (often circumscribed by an ominous urban-industrial topography).

The home itself transmits equally discrepant meanings. It furnishes the social space and perpetuates established cultural practices; it is a significant financial asset which solidifies the economic position of its occupants; it demarcates ethnic cultural boundaries; and it protects family members against the assimilative pressures of mainstream society. Conversely, the home denotes cultural insularity and a kind of bondage to a system of imported and misplaced beliefs which inhibit self-improvement and creative interaction with the outside world. Nevertheless, the home as a signifier of settlement and residency suggests that its inhabitants have developed an attachment to certain aspects of Canadian life.

Images of the family also foreground the incongruities of Italian Canadianness. Intense family relations anchor the second generation in a supportive social context and provide a strong sense of group identity. Yet interdependence among family members at times hinders the second generation from becoming independent and from fulfilling personal ambitions. Although the adult children often "rename" themselves in English as a way to express their allegiance to Canadian society, their parents continue to address their children by their Italian names. These two divergent acts of naming reinstate the differing and opposed perspectives of family members. Intergenerational conflict, according to Tamara J. Palmer, embodies the tension "inherent in the process of assimilati[on]" and exposes "the divided soul"[69] of the Italian Canadian.

Italian Canadian fiction constructs images which suggest the social positioning of the ethnic subject. The production of images is often framed by the terms of "the assimilation paradigm,"[70] and the immigrant project. Interwoven into this representation of ethnicity are images of what the protagonist perceives to be the distinguishing features of the ethnic group and the dominant culture.

One prominent leitmotif is upward mobility, embodied by professional activities such as academic study, teaching, creative writing, entrepreneurship, and the playing of hockey. These images are juxtaposed to pictures of ethnic working-class life which repeatedly refer to some form of physical labour in the home and/or in the workplace, and which imply a lack of cultural sophistication.

This oppositional imagery, evocative of a divergence of perspectives, is then subverted by the interconnectedness among ostensibly distinct norms of behaviour. Italian Canadian texts show that at times the ingenious and ardent manner in which the second generation undertakes their professional endeavours reaffirms the traditional Italian view that hard work is the key to economic success and to attaining a strong sense of self-worth.

Cultural binarism, however, is undermined by both the imperfections of mainstream society and the Italian Canadian community. The individual excesses of a bourgeois lifestyle — self-centredness, self-aggrandizement, social and economic elitism, wanton consumerism, and ostentation — are as damaging to the person as the collective obsessions of the Italian community (extreme frugality, the constant expansion of financial assets and property, the primacy of the work ethic, the keeping up of appearances, or an unabashed self-righteousness). The development of culturally-specific images intimates that there is no instance during the process of identity formation that is unaffected by historical and social forces.

E. Mythologies

Italian Canadian fiction reworks numerous mythologies and interrogates the ideological and cultural assumptions which derive from ethnicity in the new world. The recurrent use of Christian, primarily Catholic, mythology consistently alludes to the Madonna figure, as well as to rituals associated with religious practice. In Nino Ricci's *Lives of the Saints*, hagiography functions as ironic commentary, making manifest the contradictions and gaps between mythological interpretations of the world and the lived experiences of the characters. The literature utilizes pre-Christian (pagan) mythic patterns, such as the Great Goddess mythology and stories about the supernatural.

The coexistence of Catholic and ancient mythologies indicates that Italianness is a multilayered cultural composition which resists homogenization. These mythologies are opposed to, and sometimes become intertwined with, the cultural myths of the new world, which valorize individualism and upward mobility, and which are often in conflict with tradition-bound Italian value systems. Tamara J. Palmer notes: "From the age of exploration and even before, the New World has been a repository of Europe's dreams, both spiritual and material, and a significant element in the New World's magnetism for the immigrant has been the potent mythology of North America as the New Eden."[71]

The vision of the new land as a kind of paradise reiterates the image of the Edenic garden. Equally important is the fact that the act of immigration is often rendered in mythic terms. In the Italian Canadian text, the journey to the new world is invested with an epic quality: "The fact that there is a mythology attached to the experience of immigration connects it to the whole history of Western mythology. To Ulysses and Aeneas."[72] The journey motif is a metaphor for the persistent wandering of the immigrant, who is unable to find a permanent home elsewhere. Homelessness, as a trope, signifies the provisional character of ethnicity which is constantly reshaping itself and is unable to develop a secure attachment to one cultural context. The continual juxtaposition of conflicting cultural mythologies serves to highlight the shifting allegiances of the ethnic subject.

Another mythic pattern is the quest for truth and enlightment figured in the protagonist's search for a new identity. This undertaking, however, does not result in the uncovering of "essences" which transcend time and space. As Italian Canadian fiction indicates, identity is formed by competing and ever-changing cultural models. The refutation of ethnic identity as a universal category reinserts the social context as a primary source of signifiers in the Italian Canadian text. This form of minority discourse insists that mythologies, typified by an essentialist and ahistorical bent, are ideological constructs laden with culturally-specific ideas about what constitutes social reality.

The Italian Canadian textual deconstruction of cultural mythologies is connected to a frequently unromantic view of both the old and the new world. This deromanticization suggests that the two cultures are equally imperfect, equally contradictory and equally oppressive; and it is a technique that is generated by the use of irony, elegy, and juxtaposition, which underline the discontinuities and instabilities of identity formation.

In evoking opposed, innumerable meanings about ethnic experience, these literary devices preempt the possibility of closure, of fixing into place a specific solution to the problem of cultural dissonance. For Francesco Loriggio, the ethnic text presents us with "a plethora of supplementary potentialities"[73] which arise out of the relationship between two historically specific and often antagonistic cultural settings. The protagonist's search for an ethnic identity remains, in the final analysis, open-ended. This lack of resolution reinscribes in the ethnic text the multiplicity and indeterminacy of the ethnic subject: "ethnics can choose several epistemological options . . . They are under no coercion to maintain, statically, any single position . . . Only full positions are denied to them."[74]

F. Documentary Elements

Another important stylistic feature of Italian Canadian writing is the use of documentary elements to situate the story in a particular time and place. Italian Canadian literary texts tend to describe the process of immigration and settlement, and to recreate the everyday life of the characters in the old and new country. According to Francesco Loriggio, this impulse affects the form of such fiction: "Ethnic literature historicizes the aesthetic, and it is the historicizing, the reimmerging [sic] of the literary back into the historical which is its aesthetic gesture."[75]

The writers considered in this study have rendered moments from the past and etched out details about locale from personal experience and observations or, as is the case with Nino Ricci, they have supplemented this by social/historical research on village and immigrant life. The events surrounding acculturation in the new world are reconstructed to advance a certain cultural outlook in the literary text. The reinterpreting of immigrant history and the way of life of the ethnic group is reenacted in the literary texts through the presentation of the differing and sometimes opposed views of the Italian-descended characters towards the host society and their ethnic community.

In recreating lived experience, Italian Canadian fiction exhibits its connections to specific historical and social contexts. For Joseph Pivato, Italian immigrant history "has made such a profound imprint on the collective memory of [Italian Canadians] that it emerges both consciously and unconsciously in their writing."[76] Social reality — shaped by such events as immigration, displacement, settlement, and adjustment — provides reference points for the settings, characterizations, action, patterns of imagery, symbolism, and themes of this literature. Pivato contends that the "character types and the life patterns" in Italian Canadian literary texts bear a strong resemblance to the historical record.[77] In this sense, the historical is linked to the fictional; the meaning generated by the text, at some level, is underlined by extratextual events which, in varying degrees of intensity, have influenced the perceptions of members of the ethnic group.

Writing on minority discourse in the United States, R. Radhakrishnan points out that ethnicity is "expressive of different historical densities and circumstantialities."[78] The fictional representation of ethnicity consistently evokes and reasserts the importance of the encompassing social text: "minoritarian discourses . . . cannot be defined on purely literary, intrasystemic grounds: they send back neither to form as such nor to genres or styles for accreditation, but, rather, to historical phenomena: to peoples, groups, societies."[79] Francesco Loriggio admits that "ethnic literature is in our historical period one of the literary discourses that embody the complicity between history and literature emblematically. Its texts are therefore of the epitomizing sort; critical exempla, parables of the times, they offer studies about self-images."[80]

G. Memory

As a tool for storytelling, the use of flashbacks is part of the attempt to reconstruct historical and social reality. Ethnic texts reflect the "search for a usable past, for collective memories and historical data that give coherence to a minority's identity."[81] The association of memory with history serves to reinforce the indeterminacy of the ethnic subject: "voyaging, homelessness, separation, multiple subjectivity, identity as something provisional, vulnerable salience, whose content must always be constructed, these qualities are . . . the prose of everyday life, the proof of the force of history."[82]

The utilization of memory facilitates the development of important thematic patterns in Italian Canadian writing. Images of the past signal to the reader the recovery of particular aspects of the ancestral culture. This act of recuperation allows protagonists to assign meaning to vital components of their ethnic identity. At the same time, memory reveals the power of various cultural influences which complement, contradict, and oppose each other. Memory inscribes itself in the narrative form of the Italian Canadian texts we are about to study; by and large, the struggle to define oneself in cultural terms is presented in retrospect.

Reassembling episodes from the past out of disparate fragments of experience, the protagonist is guided by his/her cultural positioning in the present. Memory participates in the constant reevaluation of the significance of past events and cultural influences, and it invokes the uncertainty and the constructedness of ethnic identity in the new world.

H. Narrative Form

What is striking about Italian Canadian writing is how it manipulates narrative form to embody the plurality of the ethnic subject. *Other Selves*, *Lives of the Saints*, and *Made in Italy* make recurrent use of the "Remembering I" and the "Remembered I" narration to signify what appears to be the distance between the Canadian present and the Italian past. In alternately perceiving her/his Italian and English Canadian side as familiar, alien, and limiting, the narrator-character demonstrates a sense of being inside and outside each cultural context and as well as being between both of them.

This doubled narrative voice (which incorporates remembering and what is remembered) foregrounds the constant divergence and overlayering of cultural identities. For example, in *Black Madonna* and *The Lion's Mouth* the multiplicity of the ethnic subject is generated by the separate but frequently intersecting storylines of two main characters. These two texts regularly call attention to cultural affinities and dissimilarities, and to cultural contrasts, while the protagonists locate themselves in differing but equally unstable social environments. In *Bottled Roses*, the central characters continually define themselves in contradistinction to their Italian ancestry; they juxtapose stories of the immigrant past to their own contemporary narratives about the pursuit of individuality in the Canadian mainstream.

I. Role-playing

Another recurrent theme in this literature is the socially-produced identity of the ethnic subject. Role-playing entails both the constant appropriation of specific cultural beliefs and attitudes and the exhibiting of certain types of role-related behaviour, and underlines the self-consciousness of the central characters. The emphasis on role-playing and on performance indicates that ethnicity in the new world is not defined by the distilling of various cultural essences. The texts in this study suggest that the identities of the protagonists are constructed out of a spectrum of social and cultural variables. Shifting in and out of diverse social contexts, the characters play several interconnected and often conflicting roles.

Role-playing is represented by the juxtaposition of competing cultural role models, the ironic treatment of the contradictory views and actions of the protagonists, and, on the level of characterization, through the constant abandoning and reassuming of socially-ascribed identities. In addition, there is the use of the interrogative stance, in which the characters question the legitimacy and value of particular social roles that have been foisted on them by parts of mainstream society and the Italian Canadian community, or which they have chosen for themselves as a way to resolve their identity crisis. Storytelling is also a means of creating and recreating oneself within discontinuous and unsteady cultural environments. This is especially evident in *The Lion's Mouth* and in *Bottled Roses*. In both texts, the female protagonists reassess their social/gender roles and rethink their identities as ethnic Canadian women by telling stories about their own lives. Through autobiographical narrative, the two texts reveal the underlying and complex social forces which have shaped the gender/ethnic identities of the central characters. The motif of role-playing, like the other formal elements in Italian Canadian literature, dramatizes the multiple, conflicted states of the ethnic subject.

The arrangement of the chapters of this study serves several purposes. The first three literary texts which are examined in this study, *Black Madonna*, *Other Selves*, and *Lives of the Saints*, are linked together by their preoccupation with the problematic nature of ethnic identity. Each text, however, develops its discourse on ethnicity from a different perspective. Frank Paci's *Black Madonna* (1982) is a critical text in Italian

Canadian literature, because it is one of the first novels to concentrate primarily on the personal and cultural dilemmas of second generation Italian Canadian protagonists. *Other Selves* (1985), by C. D. Minni, represents the experiences of first generation and second generation characters. The text both complements and extends Paci's representation of Italian Canadian experience. In *Other Selves*, the leitmotif of the return trip to the old country by the first and second generation characters anticipates a depiction of identity formation that emphasizes the strong influences of Italian history and culture. Nino Ricci's *Lives of the Saints* (1990) portrays the patterns of village life in Abruzzi and the forces which propel members of the community to emigrate to Canada, and evokes the contradictions and ambivalences of Italian peasant culture. The instabilities of the past imply that Italian identity is extremely complicated and that immigration exacerbates already existing social problems.

These three texts involve first and second generation protagonists and highlight the issue of identity formation from a male vantage point. In contrast to these male-centred representations of Italian Canadian experience, the three subsequent chapters examine fiction by Italian Canadian women writers. This part of the book focuses on the differing perspectives of three generations of Italian Canadian women: the immigrant woman in Maria Ardizzi's *Made in Italy* (1982); the daughter of an immigrant woman in Caterina Edwards' *The Lion's Mouth* (1982); and, finally, the third generation Italian Canadian woman in Darlene Madott's *Bottled Roses* (1985). In their novels, Ardizzi, Edwards, and Madott stress the perplexities and incongruities of ethnicity and feminine experience. Culturally prescribed gender roles compound the female ethnic subject's social dislocation, and intensify the difficulty of inhabiting opposed cultural contexts. Although *Made in Italy* was written in Italian, the English translation has been included in this study. Its powerful depiction of the condition of the Italian immigrant woman had to be pointed out: critics, like Joseph Pivato and Francesco Loriggio, make references to this translation of Ardizzi's novel.

2
Provisionality, Multiplicity, and the Ironies of Identity in *Black Madonna*

Frank Paci's *Black Madonna* conveys a markedly ambiguous view of the Italian Canadian experience. The conclusion of the novel is equivocal since closure and resolution are coexistent with a sense of flux and change. Although the central characters, Joey and Marie Barone, momentarily resolve a crisis of identity by reincorporating their Italian heritage into a Canadian perspective, transformation remains incomplete and unstable.

The text examines the tentativeness and heterogeneity of Italian Canadianness, refuting any notion of a singular and coherent subjectivity. It also asserts that ethnicity is socially constructed. Joey and Marie are shown to be participating in the evolution of their self-images through a set of choices which demonstrate to them the arbitrariness of competing cultural models.

Irony is critical to the way the text fashions its discourse on identity formation. According to Frank Paci, "The task of the novelist, then, is to create a proper tension between what to say and what not to say."[1] The foregrounding of the opposing values and confused thoughts and actions of the characters is invested with paradox. Irony arises out of the omniscient narrator's mediation between the consciousness of the characters and the external world. It is also built into the plot structure and image patterns of the text.

The complexities of adjustment are enacted through Joey's and Marie's distinct but thematically linked focalizations. In both narratives the conjoining and reforming of vantage points is exemplified by the friction between Italian and English and by the copresence of the languages.

Equally important, the juxtaposition of discordant cultural images stresses the central characters' ambivalence towards two divergent social orders. The uncertainties of identity formation, as dramatized through the varied experiences of the two protagonists leads the ethnic subject "to cultivate a sophisticated capacity for ambiguity, juxtaposition, and irony."[2] These representational strategies are supported by the use of symbolism and imagery which emanate from references to aspects of Italian immigrant culture and mainstream society. Symbols and images are endowed with a multitude of overlapping and conflicting meanings in order to emphasize the intricacies and discontinuities of ethnicity. Accompanying this formal strategy is the motif of role-playing which suggests that the identities of the Italian-descended protagonists are socially produced and composed of a diversity of subject-positions.

Eli Mandel notes that John Marlyn's *Under the Ribs of Death* (1956) relies on the ironies of plot in its depiction of the Hungarian Canadian.[3] Elsewhere Linda Hutcheon observes that frequently "the ironies [of being ethnic] are less verbal than structural: such as the larger narrative ironies surrounding the character Marie in Frank Paci's *Black Madonna*."[4] While making salient the idea of difference, irony also is inclusive: ethnic identity contests and accommodates a spectrum of cultural suppositions. Irony presents an "awareness of contingency and multiplicity,"[5] and "questions the very act — and authority — of taking a position, any position, even an oppositional one."[6] Irony announces "an unwillingness to make decisions about meaning that would imply singularity or fixity" and disputes any "fixed, authoritative meaning."[7] In minority texts, such as *Black Madonna*, irony envelops the indeterminacy and disjunctions of the ethnic subject. Linda Hutcheon surmises that in ethnic writing "irony is at least potential in . . . anything problematic or relative."[8]

1. The Ironies of Identity Formation

The narrative of Joey Barone depends on a series of ironies which comment on the precariousness of identity formation. The death of his father, Adamo, and the attendant collapse of his mother, Assunta, which force him to take over the household and reframe his point of reference, inaugurate the protagonist's reappraisal of the cultural assumptions which have guided his behaviour. Joey is appalled by Assunta's ritualistic self-effacement and believes that Adamo's struggles in Canada have been in vain. Actions and their meanings appear suddenly to be provisional: "And he knew how fragile everything else was . . . The membrane between being and non-being was so thin he could feel the cold wind blow through it and chill his spine."[9]

The questioning of previous decisions — such as giving up the possibility of a hockey career and following in his father's footsteps — strengthens his relationship with his girlfriend, Annalise, putting his personal needs before his obligation to his mother. Although his parents had provided a secure domestic environment, their resistance (especially in his mother's case) to Canadianization hampered his development. This interrogation of ethnicity, in which Joey wants to divest himself of its objectionable elements, results in a confirmation of its power. Yet the narrative's redemptive moments — Joey's reconciliation with his sister and the erecting of a brick pyramid that is a totem to the immigrant past — are infused with a sense of flux.

Marie's story is also governed by a set of structural ironies. The paradox of the flight from Little Italy becomes apparent to her after she understands that her marriage is as burdensome as her Italian family: "She was a wife and a mother now — a mere woman who had to fulfil her biological requirements" (143). In order to support her husband in graduate school and their young son, Marie accepts work as a high-school teacher, thus relinquishing her post-graduate studies in mathematics. Through her academic ambitions, she had tried to sever the connection to a part of her personal history which, in raising her son, she now observes, is no longer alien to her.

Marie had repudiated Assunta's domineering maternalism, but she herself is overprotective and intolerant towards her son's behaviour: she reprimands him for refusing to eat her nutritious meal. Despite Marie's choice of a way of life (a choice of life that is different from Assunta's), she is endowed with some of her mother's characteristics.

Similarly, while Joey secretly dreamed of becoming something other than a labourer in the local steel mill, his familial duty, his manual dexterity, and his lack of impetuosity illustrate Adamo's deep-seated influence.

Marie's emotional outpouring at Assunta's funeral frees her and enables her to rejoin the broken circuits of her ethnicity. Structurally and emotionally, her decision to leave her immigrant culture is supplanted by a circular movement back to her origins. The images of the black dress which her mother wore and the Hope Chest containing Assunta's modest dowry are emblematic of Italian femininity. Marie's varying responses to these artifacts imply a shift in perspective. Before becoming disenchanted with mainstream society, Marie had viewed the donning of a black dress and the use of the Hope Chest as signs of a backward culture. Ironically, these very items will allow Marie to reconstitute her lost matrilinearity. They invoke the reemergence of her ethnicity. Emaciated, Marie in a black dress at her mother's funeral connects with her mother when Marie discovers in the Hope Chest a picture of a young, thin Assunta. This physical resemblance reveals the spiritual link between mother and daughter.

Later in Assunta's room, Marie lights candles and sets up an improvised shrine to her mother's memory. Like Joey's pyramid, this reliquary, a testament to Assunta's way of life, allows Marie to rehabilitate her discarded Italianness. These images of Marie's participation in a ritual for the dead as well as her visualization of her mother's ghostly presence are in sharp contrast to her past denigration of emotion and superstition.

2. Double Narration

Told in the third person and organized into numerous episodes, the events in the novel unfold through the individual perspectives of Joey and Marie Barone. The first unit of the text presents Joey's point of view and accentuates the schism between brother and sister. Joey is concerned about his mother's mental state after the death of his father and Marie decries Assunta's archaic practices. Marie abandons her mother to her brother's care and resumes her routine in Toronto.

The ambiguity of Marie's facial expression, captured in the statement that Joey "couldn't tell whether she was pitying him or asking for his forgiveness" (10), prefigures the alternation between Joey and Marie's story. Each character breaks away from Italian culture, and this thematic link highlights the problematic nature of ethnicity. The stylistic variance between the two narratives reveals differing reactions to this crisis of identity. The brother's story occurs predominantly in present time. It spans a critical year in his development, and is interspersed with occasional flashbacks to his youth. The movement of the seasons which accompanies the passing of the first generation — Adamo's funeral in the winter, and of Assunta's decline in the spring and of her death in the summer — implies that transformation is certain and traumatic. By concluding Joey's narrative in late summer and not in the fall, which would have completed the representation of the seasonal cycle, the text points to an open-ended process. The coming of fall marks another stage in Joey's personal evolution.

In contrast, Marie's narrative moves from the past (her adolescence) to the present (her life as a single parent). This longer time frame which begins in spring and ends in summer is archetypally suggestive of birth and maturity but is laden with ambiguity. Marie's rebellion against Assunta and the shakiness of her marriage are counterbalanced by her reconciliation with her Italian heritage and her growing sense of independence.

The discrepancy in time frame between the main two stories of the novel emphasizes the distinctiveness of Marie and Joey's psychological journey. The juxtaposition of Joey's story (present time) to that of Marie (the past) implies that anxiety and transformation are inevitable. Present time in Joey's narrative makes immediate the conflict between individuality and filial duty. The linear movement of Marie's story, from past to present, shows a progressive disengagement from family and assimilation into the mainstream.

This double narrative describing the divergent histories of brother and sister is the prism through which is refracted a variety of subject-positions. Both sister and brother are simultaneously inside and outside their social milieux and, by implication, their Canadian and Italian identities. As the last quarter of the novel attests, while Marie slowly reclaims her Italian culture, Joey is ready to leave his parents' home, having arrived at his independence through his relationship with Annalise, a member of mainstream society. Each episode begins in present time — Marie's disappointment with her marriage and Joey's bewilderment towards Assunta — and then switches to the past: Marie remembers her relationship with Richard; Joey listens to Father Sarlo who furnishes him with a brief historical sketch of the Italian community. Both narratives return to and conclude in the present — where the text gives Marie and Joey's reasons for failure in Little Italy and mainstream society.

The variation in speech patterns (conspicuous in the dialogue between brother and sister, and in their internal monologues) ostensibly demarcates antithetical social positions. Such polarization is weakened by the unmistakable similarities in the characters' multiple language systems. Marie's language has been formed by her university education and profession. Her ability with words is integral to the way she bestows meaning on experience. Marie employs figurative language when she describes her mother's past behaviour: "The [kitchen] table was like [Assunta's] theatre of operations and her rules were unquestioned" (32). Marie also makes constant use of casual words, such as "crazy" (138) and "kids" (147). The use of casual language indicates her working-class roots and so places Marie at the same social level as her brother. However, Joey's speech is predominantly that of the everyday: it relies on the idiom and vocabulary of the working person: "Horsing around. Talking about nothing in particular... Then going to Tony's and shooting a few" (22). Joey incorporates in his utterance snatches of the Marchigiano dialect, exhibiting an affiliation with his ethnicity.

Another feature of both narratives is the recurrence of Italian words which helps to situate the problem of intergenerational communication and the opposition of value systems. Marie and Joey's ineptness in expressing themselves through their Italian dialect inhibits an understanding of their parents' customs and beliefs. The juxtaposing of Italian and English accentuates the ideological gap between parent and child, implying that each side is imprisoned by a form of ethnocentricism. This linguistic contrast usually occurs at critical instants, such as when Marie decides to leave home and to go to university or when Joey is shocked by Assunta's grieving.

The coexistence of the two languages is also emblematic of the overlaying of multiple viewpoints. When Joey uses his Italian dialect, he admits that his facility is poor and that he must use English to communicate with his mother. Ironically, Marie who, despite her refusal to openly speak Italian, is not only much more fluent in her native language than Joey but frequently thinks, talks, and makes references in Italian: "They were words she didn't realize she knew. *'Dove la chiave del bavulo, Mamma?'* Where is the key to the trunk?" (108)

Marie proclaims an allegiance to English mainstream culture by taking on an English name. As a young woman, she modifies her original name, Maria and, later as an adult, drops the "e" off Barone, her family name. All phonetic traces of her Italianness are thus removed. Throughout the novel, Joey is known by his English Canadian moniker.

This act of renaming recurs in Paci's works. In *The Italians* (1978), Guglielmo Gaetano becomes Bill Gaetano. In *The Father* (1984), Stefano Mancuso changes his first name to Stephen. Often linguistic alienation is not the cause, but the symptom of a collision of values for both parents and children who have grown apart from each other. In referring to Marie and Joey by their English names, the text underlines the indeterminacy of the ethnic subject, of living both within and outside various cultural contexts. The deterritorialized Italian language is recovered only when Marie and Joey reclaim their

Italian heritage. Speaking overseas to their aunt, Assunta's sister (an Italian woman whom they have never met), in a language which they had considered to be childish and ineffectual, they experience a cultural affinity for the first time in their lives. By keeping their anglicized first name, Marie and Joey manifest an attachment to English Canadian society, as do Bill Gaetano and Stephen Mancuso

Further complicating the language field of each story line is the intermixing of the narrator's voice with that of the two characters. The presentation of Joey's thoughts is couched in words which often do not match his speech and which resemble Marie's use of formal English. The narrator constantly mediates Joey's perceptions, for example his view of Father Sarlo: "When the Italian priest was transferred to the parish, he was the scourge of the neighbourhood, railing against sin and stinginess with a fierceness Joey had never seen in a human being since" (146). The style, syntax, and diction of this sentence will appear in Marie's reflection on her own difficult pregnancy: "And when Michael was born, the terror of the delivery almost killing her, she was overcome with the sheer living phenomenon of him that she lost all interest in her doctoral program" (141). The imbrication of various language types indicates the overlapping of irreconcilable and complementary subject positions, which includes that of the narrator. The stylistic technique of separating and joining the voices of the two characters transmits the diversity of the ethnic subject. This motif is consolidated at the conclusion of the novel. Near the end of the text, Joey and Marie's consciousness converge and become part of the same story line. Yet, in the last episode, the voices of the two characters diverge, for we are only presented with Joey's perspective.

Each story interacts with the narrative of the immigrant experience and adds to the complexity of the protagonists' cultural positioning. In Joey's text, Father Sarlo's discussion of the cultural make-up of the first generation and of the problems of adjustment brings together two dissimilar but intersecting journeys in the new world: those of the parents and their Canadianized children. Joey obtains an overview of the efforts of Italians to retain their beliefs and customs. The novel outlines the settlement and dispersal of Little Italy in the Sault and describes the social isolation and the working conditions of the immigrant. Allusions are made to class divisions, based on economic status and ethnicity (a great many of the employees at the steel mill are Italian or of Italian descent), and to the issue of assimilation.

The transition from marginality to an acceptance of multiplicity is implied in the melding of Marie's narrative with that of the immigrant. Studying the faded photographs of her mother and extended family in the old country, Marie sees a group of individuals coping, almost heroically, with difficult circumstances: "[The land] was hilly, with every piece . . . used for cultivation . . . she saw the kind of people she came from . . . Peasants . . . trying to eke an existence from the soil" (194). Father Sarlo's account and the collection of photographs, which oppose the adult children's interpretation of their parents' behaviour, do not romanticize the past, but legitimate a devalued agrarian and working-class culture.

3. *The Use of Juxtaposition*

The perspectival ambiguity of the protagonist is developed through the use of juxtaposition. From Joey's vantage point, images of the black madonnas (including Assunta) in their hypnotic mourning ritual, the strangeness of Adamo's desiccated corpse lying on his bed, and the verbal inarticulateness of Assunta communicate a world that defies comprehension. In contrast to this confusion and bewilderment, there are images of a stable and coherent ethnic social environment. Joey is immersed in his work at the steel plant which pushes him to his limits. The domestic partnership with Adamo and Assunta entails constant renovation and household chores. Joey's passion for hockey demands a physicality which repeats the immigrant's valorization of human labour. His verbal reticence, motivated as it is by the belief that words cannot describe feelings or illuminate personal experience, privileges the intuitive over the rational. Juxtaposition constantly illustrates how Joey moves in and out of several cultural identities.

He is unsure about mainstream society, which is represented through images of urbanism, industrialization, and technology. The novel makes brief references to the density and uniformity of city dwellings, the clamorous and smoky steel plant, and the television set that Assunta watches surpasses time and space. This imagery is contrasted to the game of hockey which, for Joey, is the pre-eminent signifier of Canadianness: "hockey was hockey, pure and simple — the only thing Canadians did the best in all the world" (46). Uninterested in fame and fortune, Joey plays hockey as a means of defining himself and his relations to others. The importance of hockey is stressed through a recurrent dream: Joey sees himself gliding euphorically over a radiant, frozen lake. Emblematic of his desire for a state of unity, this visionary moment is reified in Annalise's art near the end of the novel: "[The painting] showed the side view of a hockey player with a close resemblance to Joey skating all alone over a large expanse of ice in the outdoors" (196). The dream imagery underscores the protagonist's contradictory urges: the need to flee the stifling protectiveness of home and the constraints of a working-class, one-industry town; to make creative use of his manual skills; to overcome the fear of living "in the world outside the West End" (88). Hockey permits a temporary reprieve from the psychological desolation of his immigrant and working-class surroundings: "Only when he played hockey did he feel alive as before" (59).

While the steel mill is the source of his livelihood, Joey finds his work arduous and unfulfilling. The futility of his labour exacerbates his helplessness and lack of direction. On the ice, Joey can extirpate his lingering boyish dependence: "He would play as if [Annalise] were the only one watching. He would play fatherless and motherless" (86). Yet the game of hockey is tarnished by greed — evident in Donny Belsito's account of its crass commercialism. It also breeds violence, as shown in the description of the steel plant hockey players who vent their personal frustrations and through the screams of blood-thirsty fans. Ironically, hockey is wedded to Italian culture. It demands the same stamina and dexterity as bricklaying or carpentry — these are trades which the protagonist learns under his father's diligent tutelage. The hockey stick is as familiar to Joey's touch as a bricklayer's trowel. ("The grain of wood had been smoothed down by such long use that it fit the contours of the palm perfectly" (63).) The opaqueness of daily life and the vain attempts at harmonizing antagonistic cultural viewpoints are juxtaposed to the transparency of playing hockey. When thought, feeling, and action are integrated, time and space are transcended. ("Hockey seemed to empty him inside. There was no innerness. He was no more and no less than what he did" (59).) Countering this picture of stability are nightmare images evoking uncertainty, abandonment, menace, and death. They conflate eerie allusions to the new world — whether they are of nature or of hockey — with the immigrant community, represented by the spectral figure of a worker.

The unsettling imagery is repeated in the depiction of the steel mill as a powerful and monstrous force: "Gigantic hooks the size of a sidewalk held the pot secure just a few feet from the top . . . The light from the molten steel was so intense no-one could look at it without dark glasses. Soon the mould was filled. They stood on rail tops in the pit like a chain of miniature volcanoes, their tops glowing with white heat" (57-58). The process of steel making, wherein raw material is melted down and then recast into a particular form, is emblematic of the Italians' adaptation to a technological environment. Industrialization based on mechanization and the specialization of work modifies the immigrant's labour, directing him to a specific set of tasks. Adamo Barone had apprenticed as a bricklayer in Italy with the intent of becoming a tradesman, not just a tiny cog in a production line, "a bricklayer going to the various furnaces to line them with fire-brick. Keeping the inferno going. Instead of building homes and bridges as he had always meant to" (63).

The juxtaposing of hell's fire to old world craftsmanship implies a conflict between modern industry and immigrant aspiration. The price that the worker pays is dramatized through Adamo Barone's death which is the result of physical exhaustion and chemical toxicity. The juxtaposition of a multitude of cultural images obscures the opposition between rural and technological society. The inhospitable terrain of the home village, with its hills and rocky fields, is joined to a polluted and noisy industrial city and its surrounding wilderness. Despite the rigors of adjustment, Adamo and Assunta Barone exchange subsistence farming for a measure of economic security. Urbanism's emphasis on competition, as shown in the intellectual rivalry between Marie and Richard, and its patriarchal-based social system, which, like the patriarchal pattern of the Italian village, puts responsibility for child-rearing on the woman to the detriment of professional achievement, is as onerous as industrialization or agrarianism. The novel suggests that underneath the perceived differences between the immigrant community and mainstream society, there is a kind of interchangeability of the role of the woman.

4. *Cultural Imagery and Symbolism*

Black Madonna employs images and symbols which arise from an immigrant milieu and the cultural and mythic structures of both the old and new world. According to Paci, "The writer can't be too self-conscious in choosing images and symbols. They must already 'be there' so to speak — or be organically part of the story."[10] The symbolism and imagery are notably open-ended.[11] The trunk in the novel generates a host of significations. It is Assunta's affiliation with her matrifocal heritage and her dowry-making for her daughter; Marie's rite of passage from ignorance to knowledge, as well as her initiation into a form of matrilinearity; an antiquated cultural practice and the disappearance of a way of life. The trunk's numerous meanings depend on the subjectivity of Marie Barone as she interchangeably rejects, reassumes, and reworks her Italian identity. The death of Adamo and Assunta represents ambiguity. The loss is tragic: it uproots Joey and Marie from their immigrant origins. Yet death liberates them by allowing them to recreate their identities. The allusions to Italian history and culture are contiguous with images of the mainstream (hockey, the natural landscape, industrialization, and urbanism). These allusions and images serve a symbolic function and their meanings change according to the shifting point of view of the central characters. Annalise's paintings imbue the banalities of the everyday with a sense of wonder: she tells Joey, "I want to have people see what they see as if for the first time. The marvel of it" (163).

The text's rendering of the immigrant community and Canadian society commingles realism with melodrama, myth, and folklore. Pre-Christian and Christian mythology recurs in the novel, mainly through the presence of Assunta, who personifies the Black Madonna figure. Assunta's nurturing qualities, marked by her corpulence, physicality and closeness to the soil, are contrasted to her mourning rituals and self-abnegation. Contrary attributes make her the Great Goddess of female mythology. In an article on *Black Madonna*, Roberta Sciff-Zamaro indicates that Assunta is "the mysterious, almost sibylline character," and embodies "the primordial feminine principle in the collective unconscious" that "is almost completely effaced"[12] in Christian mythology. In both Catholic Mediterranean culture and the Great Goddess myth, the colour black refers to mortality: "the black phase [is] connected with death and the underworld."[13] Like the Great Goddess, Assunta is invested with contradictory meanings — creativity and destructiveness are indistinguishable. The ambivalence of the Goddess/Madonna figure reflects the paradoxes of immigrant culture.

Within the Italian community, the Black Madonna is an icon for the duplicities of an agrarian past which revolve around cultivation, one's relation to the earth, and privation, the often deadly struggle to make a living out of a rock-hard land. The cult of the Madonna is tied to ancient pagan beliefs which saw the land as an embodiment of the Great Goddess and her powers of life and death. In Roman Catholicism, the Virgin Mary symbolizes purity, vitality, and motherhood as well as suffering and mortality. In Italian peasant culture, La Madonna speaks of fatalism, spiritual redemption, economic enslavement and moral perseverance. The text revises this mythic figure and comments on the internal familial conflicts of the Italian Canadian community. As the text's overarching trope for Italianness, the "Black Madonna" is an oxymoron: while Assunta represents the nurturer, the virgin mother undefiled by life, she is also the destroyer whose domineering ways threaten her adult children's individuality.

This binarism is undermined by the contradictions of Assunta's personal history. As a young woman she longed for the old country, but its economic drawbacks compelled her to seek opportunity elsewhere. Marriage, the building of family, and the fulfilling of the established roles of wife and mother were made possible in the host country because of its economic opportunities. The death of her husband shatters her world and exposes her to what she had perceived to be the spiritual emptiness of industrial society. Although the novel implies that she participated in her own defeat because of her refusal to become familiar with mainstream society, Assunta is overwhelmed by forces beyond her control.

Her character is not just an incarnation of *La Madonna,* as suggested by her promulgation of traditional values. Assunta is victimized in the old and new world because she belonged to a working-class and ethnic community. Her symbolic association to the Great Goddess/Black Madonna figure not only delineates her nurturing and authoritarian tendencies as a mother, it also insinuates a kind of martyrdom. Ironically, like her son and daughter, she is both part of and estranged from her native culture. Her withdrawal from daily life after the death of her husband is as much a break from Italian cultural patterns as it is an escape from the harsh realities of the new society.

Viewed in Joey and Marie's narratives, Assunta mostly functions as a projection of their ambivalence towards their ethnicity. Images of Assunta frequently express a rupture between the old and new world. This is apparent in such images when Assunta is draped in a black dress, her hair in disarray, sitting vacuously before the television set which sheds an eerie light around her, or when in the religious procession the "Black Madonnas [are] engulfed by the younger, more colourfully dressed women" (27). Assunta's terrible death expands the narrative's exploration of the nether side of Italian Canadianness. Yearning to return home after Adamo's death, she finds solace in the open space surrounding the railway tracks because it reminds her of the hilly fields of her youth. While crossing the railway tracks near her home, she is cut in half by a speeding, oncoming train. Industrial, technological society, evoked by the train, is essentially equivocal. Although it promises the southern Italian labourer and his family economic improvement, it exacts a terrible price. This difficult condition puts incredible assimilative pressures on the second generation. When Joey sees the carnage by the railway, he faces the full brunt of his own cultural dislocation.

5. *The Social Production of Identity*

In *Black Madonna*, the continual emphasis on cultural contexts and role-models implies that ethnicity is at the meeting point of contending social forces. Julie Beddoes' analysis of form and the process of subject formation in John Marlyn's *Under the Ribs of Death* (1957), another fictional text concerned with ethnic identity, is equally applicable to *Black Madonna*. Beddoes contends that the fictional biography of the protagonist, Sandor/Alex, is constructed from a diversity of "surrounding [cultural] texts" and "models of selfhood" which appear to be discontinuous and incomplete: "Hungarianness is not portrayed as a coherent collection of attributes, or source of identity, and neither is Englishness."[14] The use of irony in the novel exposes the disjunctions and ambiguities of the central character's multiple subject positions.

Likewise, *Black Madonna*'s ironic representation of Italianness continuously invokes the indeterminacy of the two protagonists' cultural positioning. In Joey's narrative, he sees his parents primarily in terms of their patriarchal-matrifocal roles: Adamo is the breadwinner and Assunta is the centre of the household. They tend not only to guide Joey but to overprotect him because they are worried about the harmful effects of Canadian society. His mother attends to his personal needs by cooking him meals and ironing his clothes: his father teaches him his trade, finds a job for him at the steel mill, and discourages him from pursuing a career in hockey because Adamo thinks it is antithetical to family values and the work ethic. Joey's dependence on his parents is personified by his name, a diminutive of Joseph, which indicates that in their eyes he is always their little boy. Underneath this controlled domestic environment, there is a simmering friction between Joey's desires and his parents' values which is compounded at times by his unfamiliarity with his parents' beliefs and customs.

The chaos unleashed in the aftermath of Adamo's passing and Assunta's inconsolable grief breaks open Joey's doubts about his ethnicity. Since his Italianness is only one part of his identity, his mother no longer acts as a positive role-model but is perceived as the other who is disconnected from Canadian society. He cannot fathom Assunta's decision to have Adamo's body in the house. After Adamo's funeral, Assunta, in a numbed state, watches television interminably as the household falls into disorder. She performs a self-effacing mourning ritual, cutting "her own hair down to the skin" (82). This not only shocks Joey's Canadian sensibility but further deepens his trepidation: "she had never ceased to puzzle him . . . She had strange old-country customs that . . . were primitive and embarrassing" (11). Assunta's emotional and physical deterioration terrifies him and disorients him. During his father's wake, he had felt a deep love for his mother: "this frail woman [who] was closer to him than any other human being" (18). Misinterpreting Assunta's actions as signs of mental illness, Joey brings her to a psychiatrist for rehabilitation. Assunta refuses to cooperate because she sees psychiatric treatment as a form of cultural intervention which will deny the legitimacy of her sorrow and, in effect, rob her of her traditional feminine role. The underlying social implications of such medical treatment for Assunta are beyond her son's understanding.

When he turns for assistance to Father Sarlo, the spokesman for the Italian community, we observe the extent of Joey's misreading of his mother's actions. The priest's sympathetic analysis of the experiences of the Italian community in Sault Saint Marie operates discursively as a counterpoint to Joey's partial understanding of his ethnic group. Father Sarlo insists that the gap between the first and second generation is fundamentally social and ideological. Although the parents have retained their customs and language, the children have been Canadianized. Peasant society, perhaps technologically unsophisticated but steeped in folklore and religiosity, has equipped the immigrant with civilizing skills and ingrained in him/her a deep-seated impulse for community: "this neighbourhood ... was ... where they could make a ... village where everyone could know each other" (159). The novel, however, hints that identification with one's social group and family does not extinguish individuality. There is a subtlety, complexity, and ambiguity to the characterization of Adamo and Assunta which implies that identity is not reducible to a set of cultural traits.

The insertion of Father Sarlo's narrative suggests that Joey's insensitivity towards Assunta's distress is not simply the outcome of an unconscious absorption of Canadian values. Instead, Joey is projecting his own despair over his cultural instability; he is torn between filial duty and his plan for independence. By mediating between the old world, embodied by family and home, and the new, represented by the steel mill, Adamo had allowed Joey to integrate momentarily parts of his identity. With the death of his father, the bridge between the two worlds has collapsed and this breakdown now exposes the son's underlying ambivalence towards his ethnicity.

Mesmerized by his mother's actions, he can see only the deadly atavisms of an immigrant culture. Older members in the Italian enclave do not deem her behaviour to be aberrant. The practised mourners, the black madonnas, who participate at Adamo's wake, Father Sarlo, and a family friend are all sympathetic towards Assunta's demonstrations of sorrow. The death of his parents makes Joey vulnerable to the uncertainties of being Italian Canadian and forces him to rethink his cultural positioning. Even the safety of family had been precarious, given the tension between mother and daughter and the repression of Joey's own aspirations. He has coped since childhood with competing cultural attitudes. His parents' presence and his emotional and social dependency on them had created the illusion of a coherent cultural environment. As Marie brutally tells her brother, "[Assunta]'s kept you as an emotional cripple. She's done everything for you like a true Italian Mamma, hasn't she?" (161) The text implies that Joey was complicit in insulating himself from the world.

Marie's conflictual relationship with Assunta foregrounds the opposition of gender/cultural role models. On the one hand, Assunta insists that a woman should devote herself to the home, to being a wife and mother. On the other, Marie asserts that a woman should pursue a professional career and share familial responsibilities with her partner. Through this intergenerational strife, the reader is made aware that femininity is a social and cultural construction. Marie, like Joey, has to locate and assess her identity within the structures of radically different social orders. The communication gap between Marie and Assunta is conveyed through a series of culturally charged images. During the feast of Our Lady of Mount Carmel, Marie, who is sixteen years old at the time, refuses to go to Mass with her mother. She considers the Church procession to be a primitive ritual that is totally out of place in the new world. Marie associates the image of "black-draped old women of the parish with rosaries dangling from their hands" (23) with that of Assunta "reciting the Hail Marys one after another, her face dark and fervent" (25). She finds her mother's devout expression indistinguishable from the faces of the widowed and aged women of the community. Marie likens Assunta's unrefined behaviour, "screaming out her name [to come to dinner] at the top of lungs" (27) to that of "a vulgar washerwoman" (27). This deprecating view encompasses all the women in the neighbourhood: "The Italian women shopping at the grocery stores, feeling or smelling every piece of food . . . Large Italian women with their dime-store dresses and huge shopping-bags patrolled the wares" (29).

To both the adolescent and adult Marie, Assunta is a fossil, a throwback to a time and place with values that are irrelevant to the modern world: "Remaining so blatantly old-country with her vulgar ways. Like still keeping a chamber pot under her bed at night. Or yelling at the top of her voice when she was angry. Or chattering like a magpie when her friends came to visit" (39). Although Assunta is grooming her daughter to become a wife and mother, Marie wants to be an independent woman, free from the restrictions of domesticity: "There is more to the world, Ma, than cooking and keeping house for a man, you don't understand. A girl has to make a life for herself" (73). Marie's criticism of Assunta's ways focuses on the unadorned physicality and lack of refinement of immigrant culture. She idealizes English middle-class life, prizing what she feels is its cultural elitism and believing in its promise of self-advancement. Her relationship with Richard Charlton, a philosophy student, and their subsequent marriage reinforce her valorization of urban and technological society. Richard, like Marie, believes that personal crises can be resolved rationally by imposing order and meaning on the pell-mell of experience.

Paradoxically, Marie's interpretation of her mother's behaviour, however, betrays not just a contestation of old world beliefs but an inability to manage her Italian and Canadian identities. Unlike Joey, who stymied his individuality for the conveniences offered by family life, Marie renounces her past for the putative stability of an urban lifestyle. Her project of integration is an attempt to give coherence to her identity, for Assunta is not the primary reason for Marie's rebelliousness. Ironically, the protagonist, in denying her feminine bond with her mother, overlooks their commonality. Assunta is just as preoccupied with her appearances as Marie. The image of Assunta in a new print dress, which "was light blue, with white flowers" (25) and the "touch of lipstick" (26) on her lips during the *festa* are connected to Marie's self-consciousness about her weight and poor "complexion" (30).

The irony of Marie's perceptions of Italian culture is obvious in her family's response to her behaviour. Adamo's description of intergenerational conflict is a veiled reference to Marie's assimilation: " 'The kids move out first,' Adamo said. 'As soon as they get enough money to buy a house in the East End. They move away from their parents. They don't want to do with their parents anymore, hey. They become English' " (66). Joey's muted shock at Marie's condescension towards their parents demonstrates that he sees his sister as someone who looks at the family from the outside, from an English Canadian middle-class matrix. These opposing perspectives, like Father Sarlo's, offer a critique of Marie's reading of her Italian community and emphasize the importance of cultural positioning.

The narrator's mediation between Marie's consciousness and the external world underscores the ironies of inhabiting a multiple identity. In Marie's mind, the images of daily life in Little Italy, especially those which focus on the immigrant woman, summon a gender/cultural orientation that she not only disavows, but abhors. This negativity, however, is directed towards the entire community and stems from her identification with Canadian society: "Ever since going to high school, the West End was becoming more and more intolerable to her. For some reason she found almost everything about it either obnoxious or trite" (29). The condemnation of her neighbourhood is presented in an ironic manner by the narrator. The narrator separates Marie's judgements from the description of the community and suggests that Marie's opinions spring from her cultural positioning. She preferred to attend the collegiate instead of the Catholic high school so that she could become part of the mainstream and assimilate the attitudes of that milieu. Popular magazines, and their values, which are sustained daily by the girls at her school, promote a reified kind of feminine beauty which makes Marie morbidly conscious of her bodily process: "Menstruation . . . made her feel unclean . . . it compelled her to improve her outward appearance . . . she had to hide her uncleanliness in a bright shiny vessel" (31). In turn, obesity, for Marie, signifies a personal inadequacy inherent in the excessiveness and crudeness of immigrant culture. Obsessed with being thin, she declines to eat Assunta's bountiful meals at home, widening the rift between her and her mother. The central character's anorexia nervosa, which remains a salient feature of her adult life, is emblematic of an inarticulate wish to blot out her Italianness, so powerfully concretized in the form of her mother who threatens the consolidation of her Canadian identity. There is an ambiguity here since, as we are to discover later in the novel, Marie's thinness ironically links her with her mother, the young and wiry girl in a family photograph. As articulated through the various gender role models which are made available to Marie Barone, the surrounding social texts oppose, support, and continually interact with each other. Ethnicity and femininity are not represented as a set of cultural dichotomies but as fundamentally unstable and variegated.

The complexities of identity formation, as in the case of the binary of obesity and thinness, are reiterated in the mind and body split. This dichotomy, with its attendant self-denial, is symptomatic of a deep-seated and continuing malaise. Marie uses mathematics "as a way of breaking her parental connection" (139). Academic study does not remedy her anxieties about her body and sexuality. Sections of Marie's narrative depict her as emotionally and sexually dysfunctional. Marie is aroused by scenes from a movie involving a man's physical and sexual assault of a woman and by her macabre fantasy about the putrefication of her gaunt body. These scenes are contrasted to her brother's naturalness with the opposite sex: "Of the few women Joey had known he was always surprised by the amount of passion he could engender in them by the slightest effort on his part" (129).

Countering images of Marie's convoluted sexuality are moments of eroticism which evoke ironically Assunta's physicality and association with nature: "[Marie] could feel her body wanting to unravel, open up, and break through in the moist, dark earth. And that her body itself was composed of this moist, dark earth that wanted to take things in and push them out renewed and engorged with life" (152). This description is reminiscent of the exhilaration felt by Joey when he participates in physical activity. The ostensible polarization of mind and body is emblematic of the two characters' incapacity to accommodate various cultural models, and is constantly subverted by contradictory attitudes and actions. As Marie's marriage slowly falls apart, she admits that the valorizing of order and logic has deprived her of sexual fulfilment and has damaged the possibility of intimacy with her husband. The experience of childbirth, her physical punishment of her son, and the connection, at the end of the novel, with her deceased mother, mark a cultural and personal recuperation for Marie.

Although Joey appears to be at ease with his body, whether it is during physical activity, such as hockey and work, or in his sexual interaction with women, he is at a loss when he tries to understand his social context and the nature of his relations with others. This sense of inadequacy is partly due to his sheltered and structured life as a member of the Barone household. The death of his father, which upturns the order of things, is profoundly upsetting for him. Forced to rethink the assumptions underlying his existence, Joey concedes that his distrust of words and the act of communication has severed him emotionally from his parents: "He felt himself choking with the need to tell [Assunta] how much she meant to him. How much he had hidden his love for her and Adamo in a stupid reticence that couldn't be excused by any differences in language or culture" (170).

The binary of mind and body, which is attached to specific social values and supported by seemingly opposed models of behaviour, continually folds into itself because the individual character is caught in a complex array of social and personal tendencies. In the words of Linda Hutcheon, who paraphrases George Lipsitz, "since ethnic and racial minorities can neither assimilate nor separate completely from the dominant culture, they are forced into 'complex and creative cultural negotiations' with and against the dominant force, negotiations that involve confronting it with its own history and traditions."[15] Marie's and Joey's narratives, then, are mirrors of each other, reflecting images of the same cultural problematic with the shared hope of resolution.

6. *Unclosed Narration*

Closure is problematized by the uncertainty of the conclusion whose thematic frame, imagery, and symbolism overflow with conflicting meanings. In the penultimate segment of the novel, the merging of Marie and Joey's narratives is supported by the circular movement of both narratives back to the Barone home: from Adamo's wake to Assunta's funeral and the subsequent reuniting of brother and sister. This circularity appears to signal the reunification of the protagonists' ethnicity, and is undermined by the ambiguity of the end.

Marie and Joey show their love for each other through an emotional farewell at the airport, but their lives are still proceeding in different directions. Marie is returning to her roots, displayed in her flight to the old country, and Joey is departing from Little Italy, the community that protected his parents from the assimilative pressures of the new world and kept them grounded in their cultural traditions. Even though Marie and Joey have come to terms with their Italian ancestry, their identities remain inconclusive and mutable. Preparing to attend her cousin's wedding in Assunta's hometown, Marie temporarily leaves behind a troubled marriage, knowing that its survival is far from certain. Although she has reembraced the old neighbourhood, the demolition of the refurbished houses is clearing space for a new commercial enterprise, the building of the International Bridge. Social and economic factors are forever refashioning the culture of the first generation. This image of flux is supplemented by the sale of the family home. The trip to Italy suggests that Marie is moving towards some new and undefined way of being since she cannot resume her life in the Italian community or continue to live uncritically in mainstream society.

This ambivalence is consolidated through the overarching image of the brick pyramid at the end of the novel. Joey constructs a huge brick pyramid in the back garden of his parents' house from which "he derive[s] immense satisfaction" (198). The protagonist's reconciliation with his immigrant culture is exhibited in the way he prepares the bricks — "Joey buttered the brick slowly" (197) — which simulates the domestic activity of his mother, and by the fact that he uses his father's "tools" (198) and celebrates his craftsmanship. The brick pyramid appears to be an expression of Joey's acceptance of the immigrant heritage.

The picture of the pyramid in the backyard encapsulates aspects of immigrant life in Canada. The artisanship of the old world, such as bricklaying, which is represented by the construction of the pyramid, is employed by the immigrant in order to survive economically in the new country. The pyramid is built next to the vegetable garden in the backyard, which is a remnant of the immigrant's agrarian past. There is an ironic undertone to the brick pyramid: the pyramid hints at both redemption and loss. In erecting the monument, Joey commemorates his parents' achievements in the Sault and elegizes the traditional culture. This incongruity is supported by the contradiction that although the pyramid is almost invincible — "it ... would be hard to tear down" (198) — it is ultimately a temporary structure: "he was making something that wouldn't last" (198). As a manifestation of Joey's state of mind, the pyramid personifies opposed ideas about the endurance and precariousness of Italian Canadian identity.

Annalise's ironic statement pinpoints the pyramid's equivocality: " 'It's elemental,' she said, grinning at him. 'It has inertia. And it's ambiguous' " (197). The many meanings of the pyramid reside in the contradiction that while its size implies vitality, its mass betrays a type of stasis. This irony recurs in the final image of the novel, in which fragmentation and resolution go hand in hand: "Then he split the last brick in half and placed it on the very top" (198). The irony does not end here, for the pyramid is juxtaposed to the steel plant, which is emblematic of the dominance of industrialization over the small Italian enclave. This juxtaposition spawns a variety of antithetical meanings about the interface between agrarian and urban society.

The pyramid will be torn down by a wrecker's ball as capitalist enterprise flattens the reconstituted village of Little Italy. Nevertheless, industrial society has provided Italian immigrants with economic opportunities which, in turn, allowed them to build their community. The planned levelling of the old neighbourhood, while it pushes Joey out of the family home, is synchronic with his decision to leave the enclave and live with his girlfriend, Annalise. Joey's departure supports the attitude of other second generation Italians who want to be on their own or are about to purchase expensive homes in the suburbs. The protagonist's evolution is characterized by movement and contradiction, for the moment of destruction also signals the possibility of change.

Through the image of the brick pyramid, *Black Madonna* encapsulates its unique reading of Italian Canadian identity. The brick pyramid epitomizes ideas about ancestral lineage, about the importance of cultural and familial continuity. At the same time, the impending annihilation of the structure symbolizes the transitoriness of Italian immigrant culture, encompassing the passage of the first generation and the modification of the identities of the second generation. The building of the pyramid is, figuratively speaking, about the making, unmaking, and remaking of the subjectivity of the ethnic protagonist, in which the past is merged with the present in an ongoing process of transformation. The representation of "Italianness" as complex and discontinuous, and as constantly being reshaped by given social forces, does not erase the distinct identities of the Italian-descended characters. The cultural "particularity" of the protagonists and the "Italianness" of the subject matter[16] remain the central foci of *Black Madonna*. Such a multifarious depiction of ethnicity is especially manifest in *Other Selves* and *Lives of the Saints*. These two literary texts examine the problems with and the contradictions and ambiguities of Italian peasant culture only to assert its importance in the identity formation of the ethnic protagonist. It is this kind of attachment to cultural roots which strongly underlies the development of narrative in *Black Madonna*.

3
Indeterminancy, Border States of Consciousness, and *Other Selves*

C.D. Minni's *Other Selves* focuses on the inexactness of Italian Canadian subjectivity. While the protagonist can find some accommodation in the host country, his multiple identities resist homogeneity. There is a radical shift in the character's perspective: "what he has met is now part of him, and his viewpoint will remain forever altered by it."[1] Marginality and ambivalence dominate the text's portrayal of ethnicity in the new world. This state "does not resolve [itself] into simple oppositions or solutions . . . The psychological, sexual, and spiritual borderlands allow the individual to explore border states of consciousness."[2]

The representation of such indeterminacy is evident in numerous ways: the use of memory; different narrating voices; the ironizing of the subject's quest for a stable cultural identity; the juxtaposing of conflicting cultural images; and the act of naming and unnaming. Although stories of the immigrant generation precede those of the Canadian-born, the Minni text is steeped in ambiguity and contradiction. The first generation protagonist attempts to build a home in Canada by reinstating old patterns of behaviour. Cultural persistence entails a tortuous examination of the past, in which the place of origin is deromanticized. In contrast, the Canadian-born protagonist is unsure of his role in mainstream society and is distanced from his ethnic background.

1. The Problematic of Memory

This unsettledness is rendered through the troubled memory of the central character as he envisions his childhood in Italy or Canada. Retrospection is pivotal to the question of identity; personal history influences one's reading of the present.[3] William Boelhower argues that "the project of ethnic semiosis, its ability to *raccontare* [to retell], is also . . . an epistemological exercise in remembering . . . its model of *vedere* [to see] is an act of interrogating various versions of the past . . . in a culture without a historical memory, where the crisis of identity and the crisis of memory are coterminous, remembering is itself the ethnic project."[4] By recalling events, the protagonist participates in a process of self-redefinition: "For many, whose history has been marginalized, obscured or even 'killed,' " as Wolfgang Karrer and Hartmut Lutz contend, "the 'reappropriation of history' is a necessary step . . . towards establishing ethnic identity."[5] Remembrance evokes self-consciousness and is shown in the oscillation between first and third person voice, a technique which is enhanced by juxtaposed images of the present and past. Memory underscores the indefiniteness of identity formation. Photography becomes a metaphor for the unstable position of the characters as they subjectively reconstruct past events. Remembrance is part of a haphazard genealogical search which results in a splintering of family history.

In "El Dorado," Rocky Sebastiano reassembles his grandfather's life from a patchwork of disparate information: "What I have are random pieces . . . though these do not make a complete picture."[6] Looking at photographs of his youthful grandfather and great-grandfather, Rocky sees aspects of himself: "They put pictures here on tombstones, and in the mausoleum I find one with my name — my complete name — and the photo of a moustached stranger staring at me" (46). Acting as an extension of his consciousness, the camera tries to recover the fleeting, lost images of his own time in Sebastiano: "I am focusing my camera on a man designing a bell of clay . . . I press the shutter to capture an image of Rocco Sebastiano at work" (40). The totality of his grandfather's history and his days in the hometown remains unintelligible: "[My wife] is intrigued by the story or the fragments of it, which are all I can supply" (44).

It is debatable whether Italian Canadian writing exhibits a clear "split" between the ironic and elegiac mode.[7] As Minni's work and the other texts attest, grief is joined to irony; cultural loss is undercut by a disavowal of traditional customs and values. This disjunction prevents a sentimentality about ethnic ties and affirms the multiplicity of the Italian Canadian subject: "[The] practice of return must not be mistaken for a pathetic anthropology, a nostalgic quest for what is irrevocably lost . . . it is not a question of attributing a lost substance . . . to the ethnic self; but of metaphorically floating a series of culturally weak identifications through a disjunctive/conjunctive jeu of ethnic ambiguity."[8] Wolfgang Karrer and Hartmut Lutz argue that the "autobiographical roots of much minority writing account for the frequent use of the first person narrator, not only by splitting the remembering and the remembered 'I,' but also incorporating the contradictions between alienation from and attachment to one's culture."[9] Referring to his own narrative style, Minni notes that in Alexandre Amprimoz's short stories, "the author writes about his younger self in the third person, as if [he] were someone else . . . Yet the man continues to be influenced by the boy."[10] In *Other Selves*, the use of first and third person narration momentarily binds the self to its ethnic other and enshrouds the text with ambiguity.

In "Roots," the central character visits his hometown in search of his Italian identity: "I [am] looking for what? Ghosts of the boy? Of myself?"(17) As Berto's mind revives memories of his youth, the narrative shifts from first to third person narration, juxtaposing the story of his return against his life in the old country: "the boy does exist . . . The boy slipped down the dark corridor and stairs" (17, 18). The syntactical intertwining of the first and third person voice indicates a reclaiming of the boyhood self as Berto pushes open the ancient door to the garden and the bountiful fig trees: "The large cast iron key, weighing maybe five pounds — I'd forgotten its size — hung from a peg near the door, when the boy was younger, he'd needed both hands to turn it in the rusty lock" (18).

This narrative instant suggests continuity between past and present: "I, boy, the two not then separate" (21). By injecting himself in the old environs, Berto releases his pent-up Italian side and reverses his angle of vision — "I, boy, wonder about the man" (17) — and describes his youth in Villa and his disillusionment as an immigrant in Canada. The recovery of the original self is hampered by the syntactical division of the two narrating voices: "He was eighteen . . . He remembered that he had an uncle in Canada who might sponsor him . . . I soon discover that the streets are not . . . paved with . . . gold; but my uncle . . . finds me a job with a construction company" (22, 24).

The disunity of the ethnic subject is reinstated at the end of the story. In the third person, Berto recalls his yearning to immigrate to Canada and his father's resistance to his plan. This passage is followed by an assessment of the old way of life, presented in the first person: "Not bad, I think, drinking Gran Caruso . . . but it is not me" (30). Like a tourist who has no attachment to the aspirations of the townspeople, he savours the pleasures that the place has to offer him. The allusion to rootedness, implied in the title of the story, is ultimately paradoxical. As the central character delves into his ethnicity, he uncovers two overlapping selves which resist integration.

Through the use of memory and genealogy, Rocky Sebastiano and Vitale Di Pietro (respectively in "El Dorado" and "Changes") conduct a kind of cultural and personal inquiry. The interrogative stance of the protagonists is a metaphor for the inconclusiveness of ethnicity. As Rocky learns about his grandfather's life in the native town, he asks such questions as "does [the bell factory] still exist?" (37). Vitale Di Pietro echoes Berto Donati's confusion: "What was he looking for?" (180) For William Boelhower, "[the] practice of ethnic interrogation . . . refuses to reduce the order of discourse to a . . . single code or cultural model and prefers instead a strategy of perspectival ambiguity."[11] This investigation results in a reimagining of the Italian past. Although "El Dorado" juxtaposes the first and third person voice to imply cultural heterogeneity, "Changes" inserts the story of the other self into its third person narration. These narrative techniques communicate to the reader the constructedness of identity. In reentering Italian culture, the protagonist becomes aware of his/her "multiform self"[12] and is forced to deconstruct highly unstable cultural texts.

"El Dorado" moves from first to third person narration as Rocky Sebastiano simultaneously relates his rediscovery of the hometown and his grandfather's youth and immigration to Canada. By italicizing the grandfather's story, the text shows that it is a projection of Rocky's consciousness. Despite the hardships which he and his grandfather encountered as immigrants, Rocky, like his progenitor who had never gone back to his birth-place, is estranged from his native land. The short story is not simply about the deprivations of the old world and the struggles of immigration. The contradictions of ethnicity recur in "Changes," which juxtaposes the main character's return to the old village against his life situation in Canada. The contrast sets up a series of adverse images that dramatizes Vitale's solitariness in Italian and Canadian culture. As he reexplores Villa S., intent on reinhabiting his past, its surroundings appear alien to him: "He no longer knew these streets, and they did not seem to know him."[13] Vitale's estrangement manifests itself in an uncertain view of Italianness in which he vacillates between intimacy and distance, as if he is observing his other self from the outside, from a Canadian perspective.

The text alternately interweaves and separates references to the two selves: "Vitale dressed again and went out, looking for the small trattoria . . . The student always ate there, settling his account at the end of the month" (174). The use of first and third person in "Details from the Canadian Mosaic" also embodies the dissonance of the ethnic subject. The third person narrative, which forms most of the story, corresponds to the "Remembered I," the adult Mario's boyhood, while the concluding italicized segments, which are given in the first person, locate the "Remembering I." The two voices point to a variegated identity which is supported by the opening and closing images of the grandfather, who symbolizes the old world, and by the coupling of the protagonist's Canadian and Italian names: "And I — Mike, Mario" (57). The grandfather figure is ambiguous for it connotes a restoring of the parochial culture and nostalgia at its passing.

2. The Ironies of Identity Formation

The text initiates its discourse on the "multidirectional irony"[14] of ethnicity by stressing the ambiguous relationship between the protagonist and the original culture. In "A Michelangelo Among Tailors," the Canadian narrator-character is primarily an observer, although Berto Rosseti, a candidate for immigration, perceives him to be an official with substantial discretionary powers. The description of Berto's efforts to cast off his old identity is cloaked in irony. He utilizes his sartorial skills — "he was ... a Michelangelo among tailors" (12) — to prove his credentials to the narrator, but, after emigrating to Canada, he becomes a surveyor in order to earn a living. Roberta Sciff-Zamaro notes in her review of *Other Selves* that Berto "must cut that umbilical cord which would otherwise tie him down ... to a life like that of his father and of his grandfather, a barren life in his eyes."[15] The deeper irony, of course, is that the rigour and precision of tailoring have prepared Berto for a new career in Canada. In connecting the high art of Michelangelo to the ostensibly pedestrian craft of tailoring, the story suggests that tailoring is itself an art form.

"El Dorado" portrays the inconstancies of peasant life through references to the town's bell factory. Once renowned in the region for its artisanship, the factory mirrors the historical fortunes of Sebastiano. The collapse of the local economy in the early 1900s is linked to the decline of the factory, while the present trivialization of the town's heritage is evident in the manufacture of "decorative bells" (39) for the tourist trade. Learning about the history of the bell factory, Rocky is aware that Sebastiano, a relatively poor town, has adapted, perhaps cynically, to the modern world. The pastoral-like rendering of the town educes a longing for a simpler time, and is set against a contemporary Sebastiano transformed by industrialization. This disjunction is buttressed by symbolic allusions to Rocco's bell-making. The bells of Sebastiano, as signifiers of assiduity and piety, recall young Rocco's momentary triumph over adversity. The invocation of the martyrdom of Saint Sebastian prefigures Rocco's subsequent tribulations in post-World War One Italy. The underlying irony of the story lies in the narrator's immigration to Canada, which repeats his grandfather's attempt to escape systemic deprivation. In *Other Selves*, the paternal figure is emblematic of the imperfections of the old world. Esteemed for his patient craftsmanship as a carpenter or a fisherman, Rocco is depicted as an old man burdened by the infirmities of ceaseless labour.

The protagonist's response to the new world is likewise unclear. In "Changes," Vitale concedes that his obsessive materialism has ruined his marriage to Jennifer, his Canadian wife. Immigrating to Canada to forget his failed relationship with his professionally ambitious Italian girlfriend Elvira (a fellow law student in Rome), he finds himself as fixated as her with upward mobility. The text signals his disillusionment with Canada by linking the bleak landscape of the Apennines to the emptiness of the prairie and by putting memories of Elvira next to those of his wife and her marital disenchantment. The ending of "Changes" foregrounds the utter provisionality of the protagonist's new world identity. Stumbling against a snowbank in a drunken stupor on the outskirts of a Calgary subdivision, Vitale sees something moving before him. He cannot grasp with his hands its indiscernible and fleeting form: "He was unsure what it was, as it escaped across the prairie, or even if had been there at all" (184). This dramatic moment, showing Vitale submerged in the desolation of his own being, personifies the uncertainty of living on the border of different and conflicting cultures.

The conclusion of "Details from The Canadian Mosaic" ironically intermingles images of a communal festival among Italian Canadians in Vancouver with the protagonist's envisaging of his grandfather mending his fishnets by the seashore. The embracing of a multiple identity is shown by such phrases as "a kaleidoscope of colours and patterns" and "the stereo of my memory" (56-57). Suggestive of his psychic struggle, the central character is drawn back "like a hooked fish" (57) to his Italian self. Ethnicity is represented as unstable. The near absence of Italian cultural codes in the new world necessitates a recuperation of a past that is highly problematic.

The structural ironies of "Gaps" break open the disparate parts of the protagonist's subjectivity. In both social orders,

Mark Lamberti is unable to arrive at a coherent identity. He rebels against his parents' work ethic and the prioritizing of economic security over personal growth by quitting engineering school and enroling in arts studies. Mark's rejection of his family is obvious in his refusal to keep his Italian name. Name-changing recurs in "Father and Son" in which the main character, unlike Mario/Mike in "Details," confirms his social distance by insisting that his father call him by his Canadian name. Equally peripheralized in mainstream society because it is devoid of images of his Italianness, he "felt he was different from others," that his "values were different" (69). Even the journey to the old country, where he stays for a year and lives on his grandfather's farm, serves to demonstrate that he is neither fully Canadian or Italian.

The fragmenting of cultural identities is conveyed through such tension-charged language as "crisis point" (69) and "culture clash" (69). The words dramatize his distress in Italian and English Canadian culture. This unsettledness continues in the story's present time frame, when, through his girlfriend's perspective, we note Mark's contradictory relationship with his family. He simultaneously disagrees vehemently with his father's traditionalism and socializes freely with his parents and extended kin. Against these images of strife, the text juxtaposes a scene of camaraderie: "She saw Mark through the window, bowling on the lawns with his father, uncle and cousins — as if nothing had happened. And perhaps nothing had" (69). Such unity is evanescent for Mark leaves the gathering, almost abruptly, after arguing with his father, to see a movie with his companion. Mark's changing moods, the incongruity of opinion between himself and his father, and the frequent switch in cultural identities underscore the tenuousness of the ethnic subject. In fitting together the protagonist's life "piece by piece, like a jig-saw" (69), Caroline implies that her view is fragmentary and tentative. Photography is a metaphor for the unreliability of cultural positioning; perception is subjective and shaped by the social context: "a picture is true only the moment the camera clicks, but just as important is the angle and the light" (70).

In "Margherita," the ironies of Italian Canadian identity issue from the text's study of familial conflict. While Margherita and her daughter, Mariella, appear to be polar opposites, they ironically are very much alike. They share a common physical resemblance, extrovertedness, and stubbornness. This irony is extended to Phil, the older sister, who in denouncing Mariella's self-centredness, willingly accepts that she has given up the possibility of marriage for a professional career. In the story, the two sisters are different versions of their mother. They mirror the tensions and ambivalence of ethnicity. Here is a story about a mother's inhibiting influence on her daughters. In pursuing a career as a singer, Mariella has unwittingly cultivated Margherita's physicality and ingenuity. Phil, who was a surrogate mother to Mariella when Margherita worked at a factory, has joined the corporeal side of her mother, her toughness, with her father's intellectual love of books.

Mariella and Phil reconstruct their mother's history according to their standpoints. The discrepant images of the mother speak of the disjunctiveness of the daughters' ethnicity. They view her respectively as an oppressive matriarch and as a caring, heroic figure. Sifting through documents (old photographs and love letters) left by their parents, the two sisters cannot acquire a complete picture of the immigrant past because it is at odds with their new experience. Even Phil, proud of her similarity to Margherita and embittered by what she believes to be her sister's contempt for their Italian background, admits that her mother's life still eludes her: "How much does one person really know about another . . . If [she] could speak, what would she say?" (85) From her Canadianized perspective, Phil sees her mother as the other. This is present in the disturbing scene when Margherita mourns the loss of her husband: "Her mother looked like a witch, hair scraggy, eyes red, face damp with tears" (82). At the end of the story, Margherita is incomprehensible to Phil: "She looked at the old woman now — silent, alone" (85). The older woman's otherness is affixed to the agonizing death of the first generation: "Margherita lay propped up with pillows . . . a small, frail old woman" (78).

This unsteadiness is reiterated in "Father and Son." Here events dramatize the contradictory impulses of the central character. As an adolescent, Frank fulminated against his father's preoccupation with economic security because it robbed him of his companionship. Frank's pursuit of power and status has led to the collapse of his own marriage and to his estrangement from his own son. Unlike his father, who laboured endlessly for his family's welfare, Frank has rechannelled the work ethic of his father to serve personal ambition. After having spent so much energy expunging Cosimo's old world teaching, he now acknowledges his father's criticism of the host country. The Canadian moment is far from liberating. Frank's life has been without intimacy and spiritual value. Assimilation is problematic since the achievement of personal freedom has meant the dismemberment of a part of oneself: "But for me the severance was self-mutilation, like that of an animal chewing off its paw to escape its trap" (95). The signification of the animal image reflects the paradox of "Father and Son." The negative portrayal of new world materialism is complemented by the constrictedness of immigrant culture.

The ending of the story reprises the ironies of identity formation as Frank ritualistically makes contact with the spirit of his dead father. Cosimo's tight-fitting work shirt symbolizes Frank's inability to reclaim his working-class, immigrant heritage. His emotionally-ridden interior monologue is on one level set off by the shocking revelation that Cosimo was proud of his son's professional accomplishments. On another level, the monologue is an act of confession, in which he asks for his father's forgiveness, and an expression of his separateness: "I didn't want things to be this way. I didn't want to hurt either of us. But I had to live and, to do so, dear father, the weight of you had to be cast aside" (98). The final image of Frank unsuccessfully trying to fill Cosimo's heavy and large work boots is infused with ambiguity. It alludes to the burden of an immigrant past, and insinuates an incapacity to make use of positive elements of Italian culture. Ironically, if he had followed Cosimo's advice, Frank would have not given up personal and familial fulfilment for materialistic gain.

Other Selves seems to imply that social forces in the new world have a powerful influence on the value system of the ethnic protagonist. The opening and closing stories, written in the first person, recount immigrant history from the perspective of a Canadian narrator-character. "Father and Son" indicates that the cultural positioning of the protagonist in the host society is mired in ambiguity and contradiction.

3. Juxtaposition and the Multiform Subject

According to William Boelhower, "juxtaposition rather than causal sequence and fragmentation rather than perspectivism"[16] characterize the formal structure of an ethnic text. In "Roots," the inconstancy of Berto Donati's identity is expressed through complementary and opposed cultural images. The text links brightly-lit scenes of the hometown and its surrounding landscape to the diaphanous Pacific Ocean and to Carla's sensuality as she runs "along the beach like a fawn, sunlight on her long slim legs" (19). This linkage suggests a kind of spiritual affinity between the old and new world. The overlayering of cultural sensibilities recurs during the fecundity scene of the southern Italian countryside with "wheat golden in the fields and vines . . . heavy with fruit" (21). Carla is brimming sexuality in Villa. The eating of a fig and her lovemaking become part of the same erotic moment. It is in Canada (Vancouver) that "she rises like Venus waist-high in the surf" (19). The invocation of an integrated and cross-cultural subject is sabotaged by the opposition of images. The juxtaposing of Villa's indigence and bleakness to the plenitude of the natural environment in Vancouver stresses the protagonist's disapproval of the old world.

Juxtaposition discloses the ambiguities of Italian and Canadian culture. While Villa's medieval sights (the cathedral and the remnants of a castle) attract former inhabitants who, like Berto, are awash in nostalgia, its picturesque/postcard facade hides the arduousness of rural life. Similarly, beneath the dream of prosperity, as promulgated by North American popular culture, there lurks potential disaster. The act of constructing an edifice is symbolic of the instability of Canadian identity. Berto makes his way along the girders of an office tower and recognizes the precariousness of his job: "I was scared, sensing long tremors in the huge skeleton of the building as though the whole rickety structure might at any moment collapse" (21). The austerity of the old world, figured in its decrepit ancient buildings and severe economic conditions, reasserts itself in the dangerousness of immigrant labour in the host country.

"El Dorado" examines the ambivalent viewpoint that the protagonist has towards his place of birth. He is transported by Sebastiano's scenery and aged architecture and a woman reminds him of an artist's rendering of the Madonna. The vista of the whimsical town is juxtaposed against a description of fascist-inspired violence in his grandfather's narrative. Such disjunction is repeated in the contrast between images of local colour captured by Rocky with his camera and the elderly man's destitution: "Rocco thought of the small parcel of stony farmland he had inherited from his parents" (43). Rocky recounts his joyful return to Sebastiano. But another story delineates the dark side of the old world, the reality which the tourist does not see.

The new world is as unjust as the old. The text announces the possibilities of immigration by contrasting the elder Rocco's impoverished farm to the bountifulness of the new world, illustrated in the allusion to nature and to Vancouver, which is overflowing with goods and activity. The idealization of Western Canada is undermined by harsh images of the Great Depression: "It pained him to see men lining up at the soup kitchen, like beggars, or marching through streets, demonstrating for work and wages ... Summers he picked vegetables and fruit in the Fraser Valley" (46-47). Such ambivalence is further bolstered by the recurring image of the tourist who personifies voyeurism, perpetual wandering, and an underlying lack of attachment to the world that he visits temporarily.

Rocky sees his hometown primarily from an outsider's perspective: "[My wife and I are] two Canadian tourists in jeans" (33). The tourist is a trope linked to that of the immigrant. Both are always in transit, always travelling between worlds, caught in an irremediable in-betweeness, in search of prosperity, which is embodied in the dream of the promised land, the mythic El Dorado of European explorers. In the last scene in the story, while Rocky's bus moves out of the mountainscape, he looks back at the image of Sebastiano as it recedes from view. There is a sense of unrelieved homelessness. Only from a distance does the town appear to be "the El Dorado of which [his] grandfather sometimes spoke" (48).

The short story illustrates the tensions of a multiple identity which are formally expressed by the juxtaposition of two distinct and interconnected narratives. Wolfgang Karrer and Hartmut Lutz observe that the minority text makes use of literary strategies to dramatize "cultural conflicts often without resolving them into one of the many directions."[17]

"Details from the Canadian Mosaic" demonstrates that ethnicity is complex and erratic. Juxtaposition is a critical vehicle for imparting to the reader the confusion of the protagonist. The pastoral splendour of the old world, where "oleanders flowered blood-red in crags [and] below, the sea flashed an incredible blue" (51), is pitted against the dreariness of the West Coast climate and the daily grind of industrial labour. The countervailing image of the grandfather burdened by arthritis as a result of painstaking work indicates an ambivalent reading of the place of origin. Mario's mother's failure to be part of Canadian society is at variance with her son's new resourcefulness, shown in his friendship with Bruce, a Canadian boy: "They built a tree house where on the wings of imagination anything was possible" (55).

The dream motif mirrors the process of Mario's transmutation reflected in the description of the early stages of his emigration from Italy, as he leaves his hometown, crosses the Atlantic ocean on a passenger line, and travels to Vancouver by train. The wondrous journey is disrupted, however, by the unfamiliarity and gloominess of the West Coast: "he woke to the shrill cry of gulls ... the bus, the ship, the train. All of them now unreal as if he had indeed dreamed them" (52). Once Mario obtains a Canadian self, the host country suddenly becomes the place to be in: "he dreamed ... of Rocket Richard or three-speed bikes or a girl named Gwendolyn" (56). The glory is offset by the protagonist's elegiac feelings for his grandfather. The forming of a multiple identity, of being "Mario at home and Mike in the streets" (56) — crystallizes the duplicities and ambiguities of the ethnic subject.

In "Gaps," refurbishing houses in the neighbourhood, preparing a bounteous and succulent meal, the arduousness of renovating the home as part of leisure time are ways of valorizing the lifestyle of the Italian Canadian. The present is instilled with the nuances of a more recognizable past: "a Mediterranean town — white stone houses with red tile roofs under a ceramic blue sky, a belltower, hints of olive vineyards and fields of marigolds" (68). Continuity between the old and new world is established, yet there is the implication that some kind of loss has occurred. Group intimacy in the Lamberti household is juxtaposed onto Caroline's recollection of her aloof English Canadian family. Against this commendatory depiction of Italianness is situated intergenerational discord. Mark contests the familial and utilitarian values of his father and emphasizes the importance of individualism. Yet the antagonism between father and son is more invented than real. The protagonist's confused attitude towards his parents, conveyed through anxious gestures and words, acts as the counterpoint to the story's idealization of Italian culture.

In "Margherita," the incompatibility of viewpoints is manifest in opposed cultural texts. Mariella rebels against her mother's traditional femininity and prefers the gender role models often associated with sexuality. There are images of Mariella discarding the puritanism of Italian womanhood: "she would stop behind the garage to hitch up her skirt, because Margherita did not approve of minis" (75). She revels in the pleasures of the body: "She had always been vain about her willowy figure . . . In bra and bikini, she sat cross-legged on the bed to paint her toes with deliberation" (79, 80). Mariella's sensual emancipation is putatively fostered by mainstream society. Nevertheless, this freedom is countered by her fixation with beauty and fame, which legitimates a commidified form of femininity: "She was wearing tight blue jeans and a frilly blouse, her long hair permed, as if she had just stepped off one of her own album covers . . . on a stage under a coloured spotlight to the screams of teenage fans" (78, 81). Mariella's sexualized self is in direct contrast to Margherita's spontaneity, creativeness, and success as a gardener. Instead of designating sets of gender/cultural binaries, Minni uses juxtaposition as a way to present the multilayeredness of the ethnic subject.

In the last story, "Father and Son," the main character is overtaken by a succession of contradictions. This short story reiterates the main premise in *Other Selves*: the exploration of the ethnic subject's uncertain positioning in Italian and Canadian culture. Such irresolution is also a predominant feature of *Black Madonna*. At the end of *Black Madonna*, in spite of the acceptance of their ethnicity, Joey and Marie Barone are still trying to develop a sense of who they are in relation to the Italian community and mainstream society. In "Father and Son," Frank's boyhood is based on the memory of men playing briscola and women chatting on Sunday afternoon in his parents' home. The story focuses on camaraderie and confinement. At his father's wake, Frank is saddened by the tragic fact that "cancer . . . cut him down in the prime of life" (89). Repulsed by the custom of mourning the dead, Frank is borne out in his deprecation of the female mourners: "the witches in Macbeth . . . old women in black kerchiefs . . . hover around the coffin and weep" (89). Ignorant of and bewildered by this ancient ritual, the protagonist mystifies the history and nature of peasant culture: "I know it has nothing to do with Catholicism, the wearing of black. It is a pagan instinct as old as the olive-covered Roman hills of Villa S." (90).

In both the card-playing and mourning scenes, Frank is poised against the mainstream, here represented by the game of hockey and the comfort of his chosen home, Vancouver. Frank's Canadianness is supported by short flashbacks of himself as a boy involved in various activities. Playing hockey mitigated the strictures of family life and delivering newspapers allowed Frank to purchase without his father's knowledge or consent hockey equipment.

Connection to the dominant culture is belied by images of Frank working alongside his father, Cosimo, at a building site during the summer. Frank's marginality persists at university in spite of his new identity (the clichéd images of the counterculture): "my long hair, my clothes" (95). The conflictedness of the protagonist coalesces in the mirror image. The presence of the other superimposes itself on the constructed self: "It's not me, I decide but a ghost, one of a long line of ancestors holding trowels" (94). This scene brings to mind Berto Donati's experience of seeing his "father's face blurred into but definitely surfacing from my own" (20). What Frank cannot make whole again, on a deeper level, is his own sense of self. "Father and Son," like the other stories in *Other Selves*, communicates to the reader the idea that the subjectivity of the ethnic protagonist "is dispersive, supplementary, polymorphic, the result of a contradictory and ambivalent 'betweenness.' "[18]

4

Disjunction and Paradox

Lives of the Saints and the Deromanticization of the Old World

As he tells the story of his childhood in Italy, Vittorio Innocente evokes a world in which actions and events transmit multiple and opposed meanings. Speaking of his Aunt Marta, Innocente observes that "her comments [were] like riddles or oracles that refused to give up their meaning, that slipped away as soon as you tried to grab hold of them."[1] Nino Ricci's *Lives of the Saints* underlines the precariousness of a tradition-based peasant culture in Valle de Sole. The author develops an Italianness — as a set of identifiable cultural qualities — which is not unitary and is constantly being reshaped by an evolving social environment.

Innocente's various interpretations of the peasantry suggest a complex and unclosed reading of the old world. The villagers are represented as the descendants of a glorious pre-Christian civilization, as vital, fanciful, and indomitable, as technologically backward, stultifying, and narrow-minded, as the victims of regional politics, and as part of a community on the brink of radical change. The ambiguity is further supported by the narrator's own inconsistent personal attitudes, which are filtered through the consciousness of his younger self. These attitudes are often characterized by such emotional responses as sentimentality, bitterness, empathy, disillusionment, yearning, and detachment.

Disjunction and Paradox 75

Francesco Loriggio states that to "reorganize the spatiotemporal coordinates [of the past] and bring into play the notion of belonging to and being away from" is "to originate [a] discourse"[2] about the multi-centredness of ethnic identity. Such a discourse proclaims itself in "tensional strategies"[3] which invoke the problematic of a diffused and evolving ethnic identity. In minority texts, the "tensional totality" of ethnicity "call[s] for paradigms that assert both stability and instability."[4]

Innocente's troubled retrospective, focusing on a brief period of his life (a seven-year old boy in an isolated mountain village along the Apennines), resonates with ambivalence and irony. The discontinuities of agrarianism and immigration underpin the destabilizing of the narrator-character's self-image. Irony is at the core of the text's exploration of ethnicity, encompassing many formal strategies. Irony is embedded in the narrative voice which continually oscillates between the "Remembering I" of the adult narrator and the "Remembered I" of the boyhood self. As Ricci himself has admitted, "there is a sense of distance and irony that comes precisely from the distance between the narrator and the child."[5] This textual ambiguity is built into the narrative structure of the novel. The "Remembering I" and the "Remembered I" manifest the multiple self of the narrator-character. The Italian Canadian self simultaneously reconstructs and deconstructs the story of the Italian other.

The presence of long sentences serves numerous functions. Protracted sentences evoke the overflow of memories and nostalgia for a time and place which appear to be irrecoverable. They initiate an onslaught of details which reveal the multiple gradations of experience. Long sentences provide numerous motivations for a particular action, and examine the contradictory responses of young Vittorio (a.k.a. Vitto) to a specific individual or event.

The use of juxtaposition advances conflicting images of the native country, and sets images of the old against those of the new. Juxtaposition ruptures the text's realism: the ordinary meets the fantastic, enabling the textures of society to hover between oncoming modernity and lingering medievalism. The text relies on sociohistorical description to present a specific ethnocultural context and expose the disjunctions of agrarianism. The narrator makes reference to folklore and local myths, and uses hagiography as an ironic commentary on the lives of the characters. In moving between various modes of representation, the text problematizes the narrator-character's position and underscores the relativity of competing cultural models. The textual fabric of the novel reveals the constructedness of Innocente's identity by pinpointing the multifarious and often contradictory elements which compose it. According to Nino Ricci, "I wanted to play with the construction of morality — of acceptable behaviour. And the values that go beyond those moral systems that society has constructed."[6]

1. *Extraliterary Modes*

Lives of the Saints covers a nine-month period, from July 1960 to March 1961, and takes place during a period of significant social and economic change in postwar Italy. The eventual push towards greater industrialization and urbanization mirrors the general trends which began in Canada as well as in the rest of the industrial world. The pressures of modernity and the declining rural economy form an important part of the narrative's background and are apparent in the villagers' constant emigration. The recurrent picture of ruin and desolation, expressed through images of old, dilapidated and deserted homes and of an over-cultivated and shrinking land base, reflects southern Italy's socioeconomic crisis. The mother's [Cristina] revolt against the patriarchal-matrifocal arrangements of Valle del Sole and Vitto's accompanying dislocation are also dramatic reenactments of the clash between agrarianism and modernity.

The novel is typified by some of the distinguishing features of Italian Canadian writing; historical references and Italian words are interwoven with pre-Christian and Catholic mythology. These various non-fictional, "extraliterary"[7] modes play a critical part in the social reconstruction of the old world and have been revised to suit the text's ironic depiction of the narrator's childhood in Valle del Sole.

In *Lives of the Saints*, Italian identity is primarily a metaphorical and symbolic construct and only at its most basic level is it a product of historical forces. For Nino Ricci, the rendering of peasant life and the process of immigration entails the reworking of mythological structures: "The fact that there is a mythology attached to the experience of immigration . . . connects itself to the whole history of Western mythology . . . That . . . is very much operative in the immigrant mind . . . I wanted to tie into that larger mythology."[8]

2. *The Role of the Narrator*

The text represents Vittorio Innocente's ambivalence in the way his consciousness simultaneously fuses with and diverges from the perspective of his younger self. Vittorio demonstrates the link to his Italianness by interpreting for the reader the meaning of what he felt and experienced as a boy in Valle del Sole. Supporting this connectedness is a sympathetic portrayal of his mother and the arresting tableaux of the hilly landscape. The narrator is dissociated from his other self, openly debating young Vitto's words or actions. Vittorio's sophistication also is opposed to his younger self's naiveté. The narration underlines this detachment from the native culture. When Vitto is awakened "by a muffled shout" which "sounded like a man's" voice (10), the implication is that, unbeknownst to him, Cristina and her male companion are making love in the barn. The text exploits this irony later as Vitto, obsessed with the idea that Cristina's woes are the result of the evil eye incarnated in the poisonous snake, ritualistically burns a dead chicken to lift the curse placed on her. The use of irony exposes Cristina's contradictoriness, for she appears to be hemmed in by the village patriarchy and responsible for abdicating her maternal duties. This double movement strengthens the villagers' opprobrium. The play between the omniscient voice of the narrator and the limited consciousness of his younger self leads to an ironic view of this parochial world.

The narrator's distance from his Italian heritage is shown in the portrayal of the severe socioeconomic conditions of the Apennine region in south-central Italy. The allusions to a golden age of economic, social and cultural achievement, evident in the references to the Samnite civilization, only serve to highlight the bleakness of the present. Such deprivation has instilled in the peasantry a sense of fatalism and forced large numbers to emigrate elsewhere, resulting in the dramatic depopulation of local villages. In deromanticizing peasant culture, Innocente tacitly reassesses his relationship to his Italian origins, imprinting his contradictory attitude towards Valle del Sole onto the story of his younger self. Villa del Sole's natural beauty — "the world seemed encased in glass, trees and rocks and circling sparrows cut against a background of sky and slope like essences of themselves" (32) — often is overtaken by an undertone of malevolence, as in his depiction of Cristina: "my mother's quiet sobbing mingling with the sigh of the wind like something inhuman, as if the air could no longer carry any human sounds, all of them smothered into the earth by the silence" (77).

3. *Long Sentences*

Flooded with intense images of the past, the narrator presents his story in long, elaborate sentences. He piles up physical details, as is exemplified in the opening description of Valle del Sole, and he itemizes the subtleties of a particular action: for example, Vitto's fight with Vincenzo Maiale. He also describes states of mind: as in the scene of Vitto's delirium, found near the end of the novel. Images of peasant life crowd the mind, but they quickly evaporate at the moment of apprehension: "the world, for all its seeming stability, was actually spinning around at a tremendous speed" (76).

The complexities of lived experience and the tentativeness of the social order prevent the narrator from having a unified and solid picture of the past. Vittorio cannot sort out from a surfeit of information what is important and what is incidental. The sensory and intellectual overload underlines the various and conflicting perspectives of the narrator and those of the other characters. Often a specific event elicits differing responses, such as the light and sound show during the village festival that produces shock, pleasure, and indignation. The presence of others induces contradictory and fluctuating perceptions. Vitto sees his teacher as friend, tormenter, victim, and stranger. The presentation of competing impulses, of a multiplicity of reasons for particular actions, and of a variety of responses to a given situation, implies the absence of a singular purpose and an underlying open-endedness.

The constant barrage of information disorients the reader and makes the familiar appear to be alien and inaccessible, and, as such, magnifies the text's depiction of the discontinuities that characterize both Vitto's personal life and his relation to external reality.

The recurrence of lengthy sentences transmits the image of a self-conscious narrator-character who examines in painstaking detail the factors which constituted a specific experience. For example, Vittorio Innocente reconstructs in several winding sentences an incident in which his father throws an object at his mother. Searching for a motivation behind this violent act, he describes from the point of view of his younger self his father's physical characteristics, the location and particular social context of the event, and his mother's physical and emotional response to the attack. After he vividly recreates this memory of his father, he immediately questions its veracity: "The memory was so dim and insubstantial that I could not say if it had actually happened" (37). The "tiny scar" (37) which he observes on his mother's cheek provides the proof that he needs to verify his memory.

Similarly, the narrator thickens his descriptions of the physical and natural environment of Vale del Sole and of the appearance and behaviour of its inhabitants. These vivid passages, which are composed of extended sentences, are at odds with Vitto's revelation that he lives in a world in which people and things are at times indecipherable: "some secret village seemed to be lurking there in the darkness, one that could not be seen in the light of day" (113). This form of observation and ostensible analysis raises more questions than it answers, also constantly fails to arrive at a final meaning. The formal trait in the novel shows a lack of certainty in the way one distinguishes the concrete from the imagined, and tends to subvert the depiction of reality. All of this underscores the provisional subjectivity of the narrator-character.

4. *Thick Description*

The abundance of details forges a heightened picture of the past in which the old world is shrouded in mythic qualities. We are given a vivid description of the disparateness and harshness of agrarian life: "why the lot of the *contadini* now was such a hard one, their plots of land scattered piecemeal across the countryside, often miles from the village; why the soil offered up yearly only the same closed fist, though the farmers cursed and cajoled it in the way they did a stubborn mule" (52). Against this tableau, the narrator juxtaposes allusions to resplendent, fecund, and legendary time: "Once, my grandfather had told me, long before the time of Christ, the land around Valle del Sole had all been flat, unpeopled jungle, rich and fertile, the trees a mile high and the river a mile wide" (52). In this background is set the splendour of an ancient and indigenous civilization: "The Samnites, a fierce mountain people, had been first to settle the region ... Their imposing cities ... carved it was said right out of the bare rock of the mountains, had been levelled by Romans, only a few odd ruins remaining now — roadside markers of forgotten import, the mossy foundations of a temple or shrine, the curved stone seats of an amphitheatre" (59-60).

Whether in decline or in a state of prosperity, the old world of myth and history is presented as a consistent force in the novel; yet it is continually steeped in ambiguity. The stirring power of memory delivers a world awash in nostalgia. This acute rendering of the past injects historical events with an aura of the fantastic or the unreal, and makes the customs and behaviour of the villagers extraordinary, not part of conventional society.

5. Storytelling

Storytelling is itself a way out of instability since, from the tumultuous vortex of past events, it locates the critical moment which sets into motion an inexorable movement towards tragedy. The recovery of a particular instant — "that beginning occurred on a hot July day in the year 1960, in the village of Valle del Sole, when my mother was bitten by a snake" (7) — echoes the fall from Eden, but does not arrest time and revive one's innocence. Instead, it makes plain one's deep and inexpressible disillusionment with the original culture. Sifting through the detritus of lost innocence, the narrator-character tries to recompose his peasant heritage. His yearning for a coherent self finds its expression in young Vitto's vision of Santa Cristina's spiritual ascension: "At last [the archangel] reached out his hand to her and he led her up into the heavens, while on the earth a great storm was finally unleashed, and the Roman ship and all aboard it were swallowed into the sea" (136).

The text's invocation of hagiography signifies Vitto's desire to relieve Cristina's suffering and to reassume a tranquil and pure state of being. It is highly ironic since it foreshadows the mother's death at sea, which is a tragic inversion of the myth of Santa Cristina. The structural irony entrenches the text's assertion that what has been lost cannot ever fully be recuperated. This view is connected to the narrator's mourning for a time before family problems destroyed his idyllic childhood. Elegy, however, is undermined by an awareness on the narrator's part that the peasantry has always been disunified and disenfranchised because of a hierarchical social structure and debilitating socioeconomic conditions.

6. The Ambiguous Representation of the Old World

Juxtaposition constructs a picture of the old world in which abundance is contrasted to deprivation. Idyllic images of Valle del Sole emanate from several sources: references to the natural environment and festive occasions, as well as allusions to hagiography, folk tales, and local mythology. The surrounding landscape frequently is adorned with sunlight, inferring a kind of spiritual ascendancy: "the sun was shining and the whole world seemed wrapped in a warm, yellow dream . . . The sun was rising over Colle di Papa, round and scarlet, sucking in dawn's darkness like God's forgiveness" (9, 58). Land is represented as being fertile and bountiful: "The wheat in our region ripened in a slow wave which started in the valleys and gradually worked its way up the slopes through summer . . . the greening of the slopes in the spring" (58, 88). Nature's powerful presence is endowed with a luminous quality: "[the wheat was] like sunlight emerging behind a cloud" (58).

The use of light imagery is evident in the description of the Feast of the Madonna, especially in the reference made to the stage show in which the ordinary fuses with the spiritual: "It seemed as if we had been transported into one of *la maestra*'s stories of the saints, the world suddenly filled with light, and all possibilities open again" (99). Light recurs in the allusions made to the purity of the saints: "A golden halo hovered above [San Francesco's] head . . . Santa Cristina . . . dressed in flowing white . . . a soft shaft of light trained on [her]" (133, 136). Images of fecundity are pervasive in the genesis myth. The villagers grow out of a giant's body parts: "In the spring, a strange thing happened — the fingers on Gambelunghe's severed hands began to grow, those on the left growing into five women, those on the right to five men . . . one couple for each field" (53).

Countervailing images, however, contest such lyricism and sentimentality. The fertility of the natural environment is undermined by allusions to its meagre resources and the arduousness of agrarian life. Light imagery is continually offset by images of darkness. Ubiquitous rainstorms and immovable clouds blot out the sun. An impenetrable shadowy world is often associated with the depths of night. Images of growth are embodied by Cristina who "stood out like a flower in a bleak landscape" (31) and Aunt Marta, "in whom knowledge seemed to be . . . burgeoning . . . like a plant in rocky soil" (130). In contrast, we are given static and concrete images, in which the villagers are indistinguishable from the mountainscape: "[they] stood still like stone, seemed to have merged with the rock of the houses and pavement, become finally themselves simply crags and swells in the hard mountain face of the village" (184). Social decay and dire poverty abound: the deserted Giardini estate in Rocca Secca, once emblematic of prosperity and cultural sophistication, is as much a ruin as the ramshackle, crumbling houses in Valle del Sole.

Although the Feast of *La Madonna* provides temporary respite from daily hardship, it cannot ultimately lift the villagers out of their despair. Their celebrations reveal "a kind of joyless intensity that bordered on violence" (102). Such emotional deprivation substantiates earlier descriptions of callous and belligerent village women and school children who cruelly chastise Cristina and Vitto for Cristina's infidelity and illicit pregnancy. The allusions to tortured saints, the ever-present evil eye, and the decapitated chicken dramatize the bleakness and severity of parochialism: "the ... air of desolation [of] the village square" (144). In contrast to Cristina's nudity in the cave, invoking a kind of purity, Vitto's erotic and disturbing vision of *la maestra*'s heavy-set body inspires mixed feelings of "excitement and horror" (42). This fantasy is a product of a confused state of mind. The ambivalent image of the teacher mirrors the ambiguity of the cave scene, which not only marks Vitto's idealization of Cristina, but also implies his sexual attraction towards her. There is an almost incestuous quality to both scenes. These two instances allude to the repressiveness of peasant society, in which sexual desire is perceived as sinful.

The retelling of the creation myth focuses on the inbred malevolence of the villagers whose antediluvian ancestors are presented as being avaricious, jealous, and deserving of God's pitiless retribution. We are told that "he caused mountains and rocks to grow out of the ground, and made the soil tired and weak" (53).

7. The Contradictory Depiction of Cristina Innocente

The ambivalence of the old world is recapitulated through Cristina's contradictoriness. She signifies the nurturing side of the feminine principle in both the Great Goddess mythology and Catholicism. The caves of Valle del Sole, where she bathes in the hot spring and meets her lover, provide a womb-like environment in which she enacts her fertility rite and releases her sexual energy. This erotic image of Cristina is contrasted to descriptions of the flaccid, distorted, and unattractive bodies of the village women. Cristina's creativity is also shown as she works in the garden and becomes part of its lush growth. The snake symbolizes the locus of her powers, for it not only moves through the ripening garden, but is present when she makes love in the stable. Vitto's mother is delineated as having a snake-like appearance: "[she is] . . . standing above me for a moment utterly naked, smooth and slick as she had just peeled back an old layer of skin" (33). The snake stands as an icon of fertility and sexuality.

Cristina's life-giving attributes resemble those of the Madonna, who appears to be an imperious goddess figure, "seated atop her litter like an ancient queen" (82-83). She is associated with fecundity when she receives such offerings as "fruits and eggs" or "garlands" (84). The Madonna's connection to spring, Easter, rebirth and resurrection underlines a Catholic view of womanhood. The Virgin Mary is an embodiment of both ancient and Christian feminine values. In *Lives of the Saints*, Cristina is closely linked to the Madonna. Yet the use of Catholic and pagan mythology intones Cristina's dark side. This is conveyed in the scene of the Madonna being removed from the church and taken to the chapel cemetery in winter time, as well as in the allusions to the snake's stealthy movements and venomous bite. The snake is given Christian meaning; the snake meanders through the garden and descends into the ravine, where the lower elevation, duskiness and wild growth are opposed to the serenity, orderliness, and copiousness of the garden. This juxtaposition of conflicting images of Eden and the fallen world is present in Vitto's mind. This is why Cristina appears both as a nurturing and protective figure and as a reckless, self-absorbed, and neglectful parent.

The binary of negative and positive femininity is countered by Cristina's victimization. The prohibition against sexual freedom is mirrored in the fact that Cristina almost dies from the snake's bite. The cave imagery highlights Cristina's imprisonment. In sharp contrast to the caves, which allowed Cristina to revel in her physicality, her family home is a stony cage. It is at home where she leads a silent and shadowy existence. Her cabin in the bowels of the ship is claustrophobic. Again "home" is the place of birth, physical suffering, and eventual death. Unlike the water imagery symbolizing fertility and life, the sea is the site of her burial.

Often Cristina is part of the narrator-character's sexual objectification of women. The scene in the cave foregrounds Cristina's sensuality and sexuality, and intimates Vitto's sexual urges towards his mother. The sight of Cristina's sinuous body leads to a graphic detailing of Vitto's erotic fantasy of his teacher. Vitto's awareness of Cristina's sexuality is stressed by references to his mother's breasts, hidden under her dress but which constantly hover over him. Vitto is jealous of the attention other men give his mother: Vitto refuses to eat his meal at the restaurant after his mother has had an intimate conversation with Luciano.

Ricci's uncertain depiction of Valle del Sole grows directly from Cristina. Here is a peasant woman who has modern ideas about a woman's role, but who is imprisoned in a peasant community which promotes social conformity. Cristina's striving for independence is contrasted to patriarchal coerciveness: her father's autocracy and her husband's violence towards her. The latter's abusiveness is a repetition of his own father's mistreatment of his wife. Patriarchy is legitimized by the other women's support of male authority. The women attempt to force Cristina to confess her transgressions before the village congregation. This ideological-gender conflict is depicted through a set of opposing images. While Cristina's pregnancy instills in her a sense of mission, expressed by her defiant demeanour, her father undergoes a process of slow disintegration: "[his] face had grown pale and gaunt ... loose skin draped over sharp, thin bones" (174). Cristina's vitality is transmitted by scenes which highlight the attractiveness of her sleek, smooth body and upright posture. She stands out in the village where women lead a deadened existence. The deformed bodies of the other village women are marked by "ruddy, swollen hands... round bellies... slow elephantine gait" (48-49). The portrait of Cristina opposes the stereotypical depiction of the other peasant women. Her childhood friends accept stoically patriarchy: "both had married local farmers and borne several children, had long ago completed the rite of passage from the small freedoms of adolescence to the daily toils of peasant motherhood" (49).

The registering of ideological-gender conflict is problematized by an implied set of ironies. Cristina's father has cooperated with the powers that be, the Fascist regime and the postwar governments, in order to defend his fellow villagers and maintain his socio-political status. He is himself overtaken by circumstances which appear to be beyond his control. The impoverishment of Valle del Sole and the pressures of modernization have compelled a sizeable segment of the village population to emigrate abroad. The community is not stable or unified. Rather, it is one that is assailed by a series of internal and external difficulties. When Cristina's extra-marital affair besmirches her father's reputation and forces him to resign as mayor, the villagers not only abandon him but gloat over his misfortune. As Cristina and her son prepare to leave the village, he voices his profound disillusionment at the old world: "this country... is a place of Judases and cowards" (175). The grandfather personifies the problem of peasant life: its maltreatment of women, class antagonisms, and economic deprivations. He is destroyed by modernity, embodied in the form of his daughter, which he has tried to forestall and which has inspired his son-in-law to emigrate to Canada in search of economic betterment for himself and his family. Yet, the old man is as much a victim as he is a victimizer: "he had always seemed a man who loomed large, who commanded respect; but now suddenly he seemed shrunken and small, as if some aura around him had faded or died" (74).

While the village women denounce Cristina's infidelity because it threatens the fabric of traditional family life and reminds them of their own failure in throwing off the fetters of patriarchy, they feel exploited by the village's patriarchal structure. Cristina's attitude towards other women hurt by patriarchy seems to be inconsistent. Not only is Cristina indifferent to their plight, she also is repelled by their acceptance and promotion of traditional womanhood. At one point in the novel, she expresses her sympathy for the Captain's wife, whose husband has taken on a mistress. Nevertheless, as the text implies, the Captain's wife's social and economic state is markedly less restrictive than that of the village women. Cristina's relatively privileged position as the daughter of a village patriarch, which is also the focus of the peasant women's resentment, has allowed her more freedom and to some extent has facilitated her subversion of patriarchy. In her inability to transcend her own self-interest and objectively acknowledge the misery of the village women, Cristina remains tied to patriarchy. The account of Cristina's contradictory behaviour, which is part of a story about intergenerational and communal strife, indicates the narrator's [Vittorio Innocente] ambivalence towards his ethnic origins.

8. *Opposed Perspectives*

In emphasizing the difference between the peasants' and young Vitto's perception of Valle del Sole, the text further develops the conflicting character of the old country. In the villagers' world view, the everyday world co-exists with the supernatural: "goats were common animals and yet the locus of strange spirits ... *la strega* of Belmonte was both a decrepit old woman and a witch, a sorceress" (162). The severity of a parochial, agrarian life has bred a sense of fatalism among the peasants. They believe that "beneath every simple event there lurked some dark scandal" (21). Fatalism infuses all aspects of experience with a deep meaning. As Luciano tells Cristina, "for peasants like that everything is a sign" (66-67).

Several sections in the novel exemplify this particular interpretation of reality. We are given an explanation of the reasons for the villagers' indigence, which reads like a morality play organized around the theme of *invidia*. In reconstructing this tale of woe, the narrator interweaves realism with mythology. He begins the tale with an overview of the villagers' current privation and then shifts into mythological time. The narrator presents both a pre-Christian genesis and a Christian vision of retribution, in which God punishes the villagers for their jealousy and greed. The mixing together of the two modes of representation recurs later in the narrative. There, a historical synopsis of the progressive subdivision and over-cultivation of the village's land merges with an invocation of the supernatural, of the evil eye. We are told of attempts to ward off the evil eye's harmful effects: Dagnello sprinkles his fields with a potion from *"la strega di Belmonte"* (54) and the villagers avoid Fiorina Girasole's doorway after the death of her twin baby boys. The narrator concludes with a ruined town, named Belmonte, devastated by war and which now is filled "with moss and weeds and wildflowers and overrun with lizards" (55). The town's sole inhabitant is la *strega*, "an ancient woman with tough, darkened skin and long grey hair" (55). This passage alludes to the savage militarism of modernity: "Belmonte... had been destroyed by the Germans in the second war, and out of superstition the residents refused to rebuild there" (54). The peasants' belief that the present is merely a repetition of the failures of a mythical past indicates the harshness of their living conditions.

The disparity of peasant life is perfectly embodied in the villagers' duplicitous perception of snakes. Snakes represent fertility — "to improve their harvest, they would buy a powder made of ground snake skins" (11) — good fortune and, at the same time, ill-will since they are "agents of the evil eye" (11). Snakes are commonly associated with pride: "where pride is the snake goes" (11). In Catholic hagiography, monstrous "venomous" (135) serpents engage in deadly combat with saints. The defeat of the forces of good emblematizes the peasants' inability to overcome adversity. The villagers invest every action or event with prophetic meaning: "people saw now an oracle, the prediction of their town's declining fortunes" (61). Cristina's snake bite symbolizes her threat to the equilibrium of the village. The downfall of the Giardini estate signifies a kind of collective degeneration.

Immersed in a primitive ethos, the *contadini* believe the world is governed by a malevolence, in the form of the evil eye, which "stood outside the normal categories of good and evil, subsumed them, striking both the righteous and the depraved" (54). Peasant culture is contradictory since the prescribed Christian order is at odds with ancient ways of seeing the world: "the eye was the locus of all the powers which could not be explained under the usual religion, the religion of the churches" (54). According to Nino Ricci, "The everyday world [of the peasant] verged on the miraculous and on [the] underworld of spirituality which the religion itself didn't give people directly. It imposed laws and codes of behaviour but tended not to incorporate this more magical, imaginative level which had been a way of organizing the world before Christianity was imposed."[9]

Through Vitto's unstable perspective, the text repeats and contests the peasants' world view. The narrator shows that his younger self is at once part of and distanced from his cultural environment. Vitto endows his mother with mythic qualities, apparent in her snake-like form while she is in the cave and in the link made between her "indifference to pain" (17) and the invincibility of Santa Cristina, who "emerged from [a large tub of boiling water] as if she had merely taken a warm bath" (135). The merging of the real with the mythic echoes the priest's depiction of Mary as both a saintly figure and a peasant woman: "the wife of a simple labourer, such . . . as you might see walking down the streets of the village" (81). In describing his elderly aunt Marta, Vitto not only notes her agelessness but also refers to the villagers' belief that she is at once "simple and yet possessed of mystical powers, a witch" (47).

The joining of polarities attains its apotheosis in a brightly lit stage show in which modern technology is used to facilitate a religious ritual during the village *festa*. Vitto sees the workaday world as a facade. This is hinted at in the references made to Di Lucci's mask-like face and the "surface smiles" (62) of the

Rocca Seccans. Underneath such posturing is a sinister and inscrutable reality, proffered in images of "some secret village [which] seemed to be lurking in the darkness" (113), and of its inhabitants, "the crowd [which was] suddenly disembodied . . . voices around us only so many ghosts" (103), as well as Cristina herself, who is shrouded in "a shadowy silence" (74). Yet the nether side of experience is often as ephemeral as the textures of daily life.

Vittorio Innocente's narrative of his youth exposes the fissures in peasant culture. The primary signifier of this disunity is Cristina's revolt against the village patriarchy. Such incoherence is epitomized by Vitto's splintered perception of *la maestra:* "[she] seemed a stranger to me, as if she had split before my eyes into two separate people: one who had babies that died, the other who appeared as if from nowhere every morning in our classroom, and who faded into some shadowy limbo when school was over" (172). Details of everyday life are situated next to a bodiless world, usually called forth through ghostly figures who loom menacingly from out of thick shadows. These images in turn are supported by a veil which prevents contact between the inner and outer realms of experience. Accompanying this imagery are recurrent references to depredation: deteriorating ancient monuments and structures, and an unremittingly barren landscape.

9. *The Defamirialization of Reality*

The tentativeness of the protagonist's perceptions is conjoined to the evanescence of daily life. Often the external world either is imbued with a hallucinatory quality — "a stole of white shimmering so richly around his neck and down the front of his vestments it seemed on the verge of bursting into colour" (79) — or defamiliarized: "the world had abruptly changed into its opposite, been completely overturned" (121).

The defamiliarization of external reality is strengthened by the superimposition of exotic or fantastic images onto descriptions of ruin and decay, evident in the eerie and exaggerated representation of the Giardini estate. This disorientation is induced by the use of jarring analogies, such as Cristina's father's withdrawal from village life: "Over [his] face a film had formed, tangible as stone, which he retreated behind like a snail into its shell" (57). There is an instability to existence which makes any form of human endeavour appear superficial and inconsequential: "you had only to turn your back and the glitter would fade" (62). Reality can be apprehended only as flux, as impermanence: "the market in Rocca Secca seemed real, at least honest in its transience" (62). The ephemerality of the market place stands as a metaphor for the construction of social reality: "[the market] had been carted in . . . and by afternoon it would be faded and finished . . . the stalls boarded up until the following day" (62). This view is revisited later in the novel when Vitto becomes startled by the incongruity between technology and medievalism: "the . . . equipment . . . looked strange and unreal, like something that had no connection to the square or the people gathered there, that might have descended suddenly from the sky to impose itself among us" (93). In juxtaposing images of modernization to those of pre-industrial society, the text suggests the constant reframing of reality. The act of electrical wizardry temporarily transforms Villa del Sole's stony and ancient square "into a pocket of rich modernity" (99).

The slipperiness of Vitto's apprehension of reality — experience is fleeting and rarefied — communicates the inconstancies of peasant culture and, thus, the impossibility of reconstituting an essential Italianness. The intangibility of human action is recapitulated in the villagers' subjective interpretation of Cristina's social defiance: "It was as if my mother had simply written a character in the air, a cipher, and those who looked on it were happy enough to give it the meaning that suited them" (142). As Innocente reinhabits his other self, his mind fills with contorted images of peasant life: "the world looked oddly warped and unstable, like something seen through a piece of curved glass . . . all the events of the afternoon beginning to distort and skew like objects in a curved mirror" (47, 127). These glass and mirror images not only express Vitto's confusion and displacement but also, and more importantly, evoke a fragmented Italian identity. Like aunt Marta, who wavers "between nonsense and lucidity" (131), Innocente reconfigures from out of the disparate materials of memory a sometimes revelatory but relentlessly unsteady picture of the immigrant past.

In joining dream to lived experience, the text deepens its study of the uncertainties of the Italian Canadian subject. Not only do dreams reenact actual moments in time — "strange images troubled me . . . Father Nick standing solemnly before a coffin in the church, reciting a mass for Mr. Mario Gallino" (116) — but so does reality manifest itself through reverie: "remembering that I was in my bare feet and undershirt I felt suddenly ashamed, like in dreams I had where I found myself inexplicably naked in school or in church" (22). There appears to be no firm ground that forms reality. Daily activity is repeatedly indistinguishable from Vitto's unconscious. The fusing of dream and reality mirrors the peasants' sense of the world and reveals Vitto's troubled relations with his fellow villagers and family, as well as his subsequent trauma of immigration. Disturbing images of past events infiltrate Vitto's unconscious. The bloody corpse of a chicken implies an incapacity to protect his mother from the malice of the village. Vitto's terror over Cristina's pregnancy arises from his fear that she will give birth to a snake-headed child, "some new demon took possession of her" (110), and from a haunting dream of her hatching a "large blue egg" (119).

Vitto's journey is presented as a kind of mirage, signifying the marvel and strangeness of immigration. Features of his trip — the shoreline, "a dusty sun-drenched town of white adobe" (202), the sea, which stretched "away in every direction, it seemed, to the very ends of the earth" (204), and the bowels of the ship, where "everything seemed larger than life, as if made by giants" (203) — are suffused with an intensity and vivacity which dramatize Vitto's whimsical and child-like view of the world. The journey itself proves to be nightmarish. Vitto's frightening encounter with the sea is framed in fantastical terms: "for a moment it seemed the world had obeyed me . . . [and had] give[n] me time to crawl into the sea's belly and find whatever spoils of storms and tempests lay half-digested there" (219). The force of the waves knocks him against a stairwell, rendering him unconscious: "Then as if in a dream the wave finally closed over me, and the world went black" (219). The brutality of the storm foreshadows Vitto's tragic and final break from Valle del Sole. Relieved by the birth of his baby sister, whose human shape erases his dread of the evil eye, Vitto sees a wondrous world, disclosed in the image of the evening sky: "a thousand stars glinting overhead" (22). Yet his victory over the powers of darkness (embodied by the storm) is short-lived. Vitto moves between wakefulness and dream as his mother bleeds profusely. The eeriness of the scene invokes Vitto's incredulity and terror.

Cristina's death throws him into a state of delirium. Confusion, incoherence, and hallucination mark his psychological separation from the old world (represented by the ship) and the new (signalled by the presence of his father). Vitto's delirium symbolically calls attention to the provisionality of Italian Canadian identity. It is made obvious by the sense of dreadfulness that pervades the depictions of both the old and new world. Images of Canada's forbidding natural environment reproduce the narrator's rendering of the rocky and arid landscape of Valle del Sole.

The overlayering of the real on the numinous and irrational, and the affiliation of dream with reality sabotage any notion that there exists a solid referential universe outside human consciousness. Vittorio Innocente's contradictory reexploration of his Italian childhood destabilizes "the fixity of origins."[10] Italian Canadian writers, such as Ricci, Paci and Minni, deconstruct "images of fixity" by continually focusing on the discontinuities within and between two separate and often adverse cultural perspectives.[11] *Lives of the Saints*, *Black Madonna*, and *Other Selves* invoke the conflictedness of the culture of origin and present a precarious reading of ethnicity. This instability is evident in the way the three texts describe the protagonists' ambivalent view of (and their difficult experiences in) Canadian industrial-urban society.

10. Immigration and the Ambivalent Portrayal of the New World

In *Lives of the Saints*, the new world imparts a sense of disjunction: "America. How many dreams and fears and contradictions were tied up in that single word . . . some said [Canada] was a vast cold place with rickety wooden houses and great expanses of bush and snow, others a land of flat green fields that stretched for miles and of lakes as wide as the sea, an unfallen world without mountains or rocky earth" (160, 162). This passage seethes with irony, for while it harks back to the privations in the old country, its countervailing images of fertility and bountifulness betray the immigrant's attempt to regain a lost paradise which "shimmered just beneath the surface of the seen" (162).

Immigration to North America is perceived to be a way out of the ferment and incoherence of southern Italy. The act of mythification, in which "America . . . [was] more a state of mind than a place" (162), is quickly undermined by allusions to unrelenting hardship: "sooty factories and back-breaking work and poor wages and tiny bug-infested shacks" (162). The wasteland imagery of industrial society evokes the dark side of the Sun Parlour, a shadowy world not unlike that of Valle del Sole. The interchangeability of the two places is ironically underlined by the similarity of their names. The new world perpetuates the injustices and miseries of the old: "America . . . continued merely the mundane life which the peasants accepted as their lot, their fate, the daily grind of toil without respite" (162).

The fragmented story of Vitto's father restates the contradictions of both Canada and rural Italy. References to his indecipherable letters and mysterious life in the new world elicit a disembodied figure, whom Vitto "sometimes imagined . . . had no face at all, merely a shadowy blank that hid him from the world like a veil" (36). Mario Innocente personifies the inadequacies of a male-centred peasant society. He is depicted as a tyrannical and violent man who physically abused his wife, Cristina, and who still controls the lives of his family from afar. He tells his wife that she and her son should no longer sleep in the same bed. The indictment of the father is mitigated by the sending of a part of his earnings to Cristina so that she and Vitto can be economically stable. The text's account of Innocente's immigration to Canada, nevertheless, is highly ambivalent. After being laid off from his factory job, Innocente is compelled to do menial work on a farm in order to make ends meet. He lives in a refurbished room next to the barn, which Cristina sarcastically refers to as "a chicken coop" (94). Although Mario Innocente can always find some form of employment in Canada, the working conditions there are as burdensome as those in Valle del Sole.

There is an ambiguity to the narrator-character's representation of Canadian and Italian society. The trauma of emigration, in which "it seemed [mother and son] were being ripped untimely from [their] womb" (164), is as hurtful as Vitto's social ostracism in the village. The reference to the womb is doubly ironic since it recalls Vitto's moment of joy and unity with his mother in the cave. Immigration, then, signifies not only that the new world is fundamentally undefined terrain — "a kind of limitless space" (165). The old country remains ingrained in the consciousness of the immigrant. According to the narrator, Vitto was on "a journey . . . that took direction not from its destination but from its point of departure, Valle del Sole, which somehow could not help but remain always visible on the receding shore" (165).

The conclusion of the novel centres on Cristina's death. Here is invoked the demise of the old way of life: "The words of a song were floating into my head, surfacing like sunken relics from a place that was no longer visible on the horizon, that had been swallowed into the sea" (237). Such nullification is in marked contrast to earlier images of the liberating journey. The narrative is drenched in allusions to the natural elements: "the air and sun seemed to bring back to my mother a warm radiance, as if the crisp blue of the sky and sea had seeped inside of her . . . around us the sea lay bright blue and placid" (202, 204). Instead of symbolically acting as a bridge to the new land, the ocean metaphorically entombs the old culture as Cristina is buried at sea. As Ricci has observed, "'while immigration is providing this escape, it is also destroying a certain way of life.'"[12] When Vitto finally arrives in Canada, he finds an inhospitable place — "we rolled across a desolate landscape, bleak and snow-covered" (234) — totally at odds with the mythic America promised by the peasants. The old world lingers on. It persists as ethnic identity in the new. But it soon becomes Vitto's final, dark view of Valle del Sole: "the villagers — some of them had begun to move now, drifting like wraiths towards the edge of town" (184). This picture of ruin will finally reinforce Vitto's avowed desire to break from his Italian culture. His relationship with a fellow village boy, Fabrizio, now is transmitted through images of entrapment and self-mutilation: "I hated him . . . as if he were something shackled to me that I must cut away at all costs, the way animals gnawed off their own limbs when caught in a hunter's trap" (127). Fabrizio is socially and economically marginalized and he reminds Vitto of the imperfections of the old world.

11. The Ironic Treatment of the Story of Santa Cristina

The interweaving of the stories of Cristina and Santa Cristina discloses the ironies and contradictions of village life in Abruzzi. Cristina's opposition to a conformist and patriarchal social system is linked to her saintly counterpart's scorning of the materialism and idolatry of Roman civilization. (In both stories, the paternal figure is characterized as oppressive and spiritually sterile.) As a result of their iconoclasm, the two women are made to undergo "a long series of chastisements" (135), typified by brutal torture or social ostracism.

The interrelation between the mythic and the "real" further manifests itself through references to physical endurance. The menacing presence of a snake/serpent and the light imagery respectively suggest purity, salvation, and blessedness. The text's reworking of hagiography — of the veneration of the Roman Cristina — privileges an emancipated womanhood. The sheer force of Santa Cristina's presence evokes a selfless but powerful femininity. This evocation reinforces the image of Cristina as a sexually and emotionally liberated woman who defies the dictates of patriarchy. The use of the story of Santa Cristina underlines the gap between myth and reality. Despite the extremity of her predicament and the wickedness of Roman civilization, Santa Cristina achieves spiritual transcendence and immortality. In contrast, Cristina's life appears to be empty of such redemption, for even the birth of a daughter, which signifies feminine continuity, does not alleviate the tragedy of her death.

For Cristina, America connotes a place where individuality takes precedence over collective duty and she appears to act out the villagers' hidden desires. On the eve of her departure for Canada, Cristina berates her fellow villagers for their lack of independence: "not one of you knows what it means to be free and make a choice" (184). Vitto innocently accepts his mother's criticism of Valle del Sole and sees the journey to the new world as an act of liberation: "all that could ever cause pain and harm was being left behind on the receding shore, and my mother and I would melt now into an endless freedom as broad and as blue as the sea" (201). This statement is ironic, for Cristina's decision to emigrate is based on the belief that the new world will provide a better nurturing environment for her son and soon-to-be-born child.

Immigration reasserts the importance of family in Cristina's life. However, as her death attests, the immigrant is not immune to the damaging effects of the ancestral culture, organized around an inflexible patriarchal social order. Ultimately, the story of Santa Cristina's altruism and salvation is out of step with Vitto's experiences in the Apennines and his traumatic immigration to Canada. Cristina's tragic death at sea functions as an ironic inversion of Santa Cristina's ascension. Cristina, not her tormentors, gets swallowed up by the sea. Santa Cristina's self-abnegation allows her entry into paradise, yet Cristina Innocente is punished for affirming her individuality. Unlike the angels in the Christian fable, Darcangelo, the captain's assistant, who attends to Cristina's needs on the ship, does not rescue her from impending doom.

12. Lack of Narrative Closure

The conclusion of *Lives of the Saints* confirms the ironic and ambivalent character of Vittorio Innocente's narrative. As Vitto's lucky lira slips out of his hand and tumbles into the sea, the text repeats the opening image in the novel in which the reenactment of the past is presented in metaphorical terms, through the evocation of water imagery: "If this story has a beginning, a moment at which a single gesture broke the surface of events like a stone thrown into the sea . . ." (7). The use of the qualifier "If" indicates that the narrator implicitly questions his attempt to reduce the details of personal history to a specific incident. In doing so, he emphasizes not just the arbitrariness of his tale but an inability to fashion from the dynamic of lived experience a whole picture of the past. He perceives personal history to be essentially unclosed, without final resolution or resting point: "the ripples cresting endlessly" (7).

The lira sinks into the swirling vortex of the sea as a stone puncturing the water's surface and symbolically brings the ending and the beginning of the story together. This intimating of a circular movement highlights the narrator's act of remembering. The two images respectively initiate and conclude his storytelling. The text problematizes such closure by constructing an ambiguous and, ultimately, grim picture of immigration. The lira (a talisman of the old world) is unable to protect Vitto from misfortune and cannot provide him with any sign which will redeem his tragic journey to Canada. While he looks intently at the rolling coin, searching for "some final secret message, some magic consolation" (238), it "tilt[s] fatally towards the rails . . . tumbling out to the sea" (238). The image both symbolically redramatizes Cristina's burial and reiterates the passage of the old way of life.

The text's ironic and elegiac representation of the old world is magnified by the terrible in-betweenness of Vitto's existence. In the final moments of the narrative, he remains suspended between two worlds, one that has disappeared from view but which still haunts his consciousness and another which, while it is near, is beyond his reach. *Lives of the Saints* portrays Vitto's cultural dislocation in the way that it moves from Cristina's burial to glimpses of his father and the Canadian landscape and back to the Saturnia where Vitto is recovering from his delirium.

This circular movement recapitulates the overall narrative thrust of the novel whose gaze is turned backward. In focussing on the act of crossing over, rather than on embarkation or settlement in the new world, the text calls attention to the transience and indeterminacy of the immigrant and, by implication, to cultural transformation. Unlike the ending of the story of Santa Cristina, which evokes victory over evil and human suffering, the conclusion of the novel is suffused with a sense of loss which preempts any form of redemption. It also ironically reminds us of the peasants' amoral vision of life: evil strikes both the wicked and the righteous. This remembering of Vitto's Italian past is characterized by unrelenting ambiguity and irony. The text's ironic use of point of view and mythology, whether pre-Christian or Catholic, breaks open the cultural-ideological contradictions of the old world and signals to us the disjunctions within the consciousness and narrative of Vittorio Innocente.

5

Discontinuity and Femininity

Made in Italy's Contestation of Italian Patriarchy

Maria Ardizzi's *Made in Italy* concentrates on the issue of gender and the ways that a woman's role in immigrant and mainstream society shapes her personal and cultural identity. Unlike the previous books in which the emphasis was primarily on the reframing of cultural perspectives, *Made in Italy* explores the feminine dimensions of ethnicity and actively scrutinizes the patriarchal assumptions of the Italian immigrant family. The novel investigates the female subject's accommodation to, and refutation of, a largely male-centred culture.

This feminine reading of ethnicity recurs in *The Lion's Mouth* and *Bottled Roses* which deal respectively with second and third generation Italian Canadian women, and recount the difficulties of asserting one's feminine identity in the face of two patriarchally-based cultures. In *Made in Italy*, the protagonist's struggle towards self-actualization is much more intense than it is in *The Lion's Mouth* or in *Bottled Roses* because, unlike the female characters in these other two texts, she is situated almost exclusively within the traditional Italian family structure.

Franca Iacovetta claims that immigration for the Italian woman has been discordant: "Women . . . derived tremendous self-satisfaction from their labours and they . . . saw themselves as indispensable to the family. But one cannot ignore the special strains on women's lives and the kinds of gender-specific abuse and exploitation that can wreak irreparable psychological and physical havoc on women's lives."[1] Canada offered the immigrant woman a set of social and economic alternatives, alternatives which were not necessarily superior to those in the old country. Immigration exacerbated "the complex [and at times antagonistic] power relations within the Italian immigrant family."[2] Helen Barolini contends that "more than for men, the displacement from one culture to another represented a real crisis of identity for the Italian woman" who was "caught in the clash between tradition and her own self-fulfilment."[3] The new world perpetuates and tragically compounds the gender strife in the old.

Through its invocation of the multi-faceted reality of the ethnic subject, *Made In Italy* "interprets the experiences of [the immigrant] past and brings into view what had been inexplicable, painful, dubious, conflicting."[4] Ethnicity and femininity are influenced by competing, contradictory, and interconnected social and cultural contexts. Irony and juxtaposition invoke the disjunctions and indeterminacy of the Italian-descended female protagonist. Reinforcing this complex reading of ethnicity is the use of elegy which intimates both cultural loss and disillusionment with the parochial culture.

The juxtaposing of story lines highlight the various positions of the characters from cultural separateness to forms of integration and assimilation. These many alternatives connected with acculturation are manifested through "different characters, different kinds of choices, [and] different mental states and stresses as they appear in the novel."[5]

Maria Ardizzi notes in the preface of her novel that "the characters are creations of the imagination; although they are embedded in the real world . . . [they] have become symbols of a cultural milieu."[6] In contrasting the depictions of the old and new world articulated through images and motifs of male and female space, this novel reveals the tensions within the protagonist's manifold and discontinuous self.

1. *First Person Narration*

The subjective point of view in the novel stems from the fact that Nora Moratti is both the narrator and the central protagonist of her story. However, Maria Ardizzi's use of irony counters this lack of self-critical distance. Irony reveals the gaps between Nora Moratti's words and actions and fissures the ostensible unity of her narrative. This disunity points to the unreliability of her autobiography and underlines the limitations of her cultural/gender perspective.

The contradictions of Nora Moratti's personality arise in her interaction with the other characters. Although she recognizes Jane's right to claim her son, just as she had done with her husband, Nora discourages Matteo from continuing the relationship. She criticizes Andrea's obsessive striving for socioeconomic status and his neglect of Peggy. Yet Andrea's deportment and treatment of his wife repeat the pattern of Nora's troubled marriage with Vanni. Nora's criticism is further undercut by her insistence that Andrea should check his adulterous wife's behaviour. The protagonist's advocacy of feminine autonomy is supported by the value system of the new world and is at variance with the ways that patriarchal-matrifocal tradition forestalls such individuality.

First person narration exposes the instability of ethnic subjectivity through the overlapping of memory and experience, of vision and nightmare, of past and present, and of the old and new culture. Nora's confessions prefigure the moral ambiguity and epistemological uncertainty of forging a new world identity. The protagonist summons an evanescent and imperturbable universe, and refuses to make a final judgement on the lives of others. She avers that people are the architects of their own destiny: "Each one of us has an appointment with himself" (156). Reference to the masculine (in enunciating the universality of experience) demonstrates the degree to which patriarchal culture has moulded Nora's view of the world. She recites past sins and addresses an abstract God who does not lessen her anguish. On the contrary, this only intensifies her self-consciousness and confusion. Nora's act of confession is duplicitous because, although she states that "at my age life has no secrets" (4), her narrative is a compendium of unspoken desires, fears, and repressed feelings of guilt: "The flow of life is full of hidden, tormented . . . pleading sounds" (5). There is no unified identity, but instead a series of guises, roles, and attitudes which often contest and sabotage one another.

2. *Silence*

Silence is a primary signifier of cultural incoherence. The text is filled with many references to silence: "my silence must... seem inhuman" (35), "the vast silent world" (205), "from my silent distance" (213). As the protagonist realizes that "beneath the enigmatic smile playing on [Michele's] lips... I divined the malignant urgency of other words" (135), the reader observes the narrator-protagonist often lapsing into silence. She suppresses information about herself in an effort to contain her anxiety and panic over the alteration of Italian immigrant culture. The shock of Matteo's murder severs her only link to the outside world, her family and mainstream society. The murder renders her completely speechless. Nora's paralysis causes her to lose her voice and is part of the trauma of translocation. What underlies her silence is the experience of gender oppression in the old world. In response to her father's dictates that she leave school to devote herself to household chores and prepare herself for marriage, young Nora is "lost and speechless as if the world had suddenly closed before [her]" (26). Also, she is dumbfounded by her husband's physical and sexual assault: "I feared him... the words I would have liked to say died on my lips" (62). Silence is itself symbolic of the subjectivity and mutability of immigration and adaptation: "I do not speak... to each the privilege of arriving... at his own destination" (5). The suggestion that ethnicity is provisional undermines Nora's attempt to historically document her life through her narrative.

Connected to the motif of silence is the problem with communication. The ideological antagonisms in the new world block verbal interaction between Nora and members of her family. In Toronto, the protagonist has a measure of freedom from her husband by working at a local factory, but she is forced to sustain the traditional values of placing hard work and familial duty before material and personal fulfilment.

Vanni renames himself John as a way to illustrate his allegiance to urban-capitalist society. He is the antithesis of his wife. Driven by his need to build an empire, John (Vanni) neglects his children and accelerates the breakdown of his marriage. There is virtually no verbal exchange between Vanni and Nora. Nora is ineffective when she tries to make contact in English with her Canadian neighbours: "I could not find the words to speak" (98). The failure of language, the uselessness of words, underline the extent of Nora's estrangement from her adult children. This is epitomized in Nora's inability to communicate with Matteo, her Canadianized son: "If only I could find the courage to put some precise questions to him" (69).

3. Memory

The use of memory seems to provide the material for documenting and understanding the patterns of cultural and personal history: "My memory is a storehouse into which events have been crammed like belongings into closets . . . as I recall [events], each is a link in the chain which brings me back to the present . . . In my remembering there is . . . only an honest commitment to understand what I have not entirely understood, to seek an answer" (2, 50). Remembrance, however, entails the arbitrary reordering of selected memories into a discernible pattern: "I discard much that is useless . . . I encounter events that . . . have left a mark" (49). It also necessitates the reinterpretation of the meaning of lived experience: "my mind loses itself in an all-consuming reconstruction of that night" (203). The imagining of the past insinuates that identity is a personal and social construct. Memories send back images of a conflicted individual who is simultaneously assuaged and tormented by the past. While Nora vouches for the liberating power of memory, she realizes that "memories are like incurable ills" (96). Remembrance is fundamentally contradictory, since memories are presented as being alternately permanent ("Memories don't die like people do" [116]), unfixed ("The faces I love appear before me foggy and unreachable" [156]), and infinitely perishable: "Time has provided only for the destruction of memories" (205-206).

The unsteadiness and contradictoriness of memory hint at an irrepressible ambiguity about ethnicity in the new world: "Episodes which are lived and cemented in the flesh. Good and evil, pleasure and sorrow, black and white . . . never separated, never left half-way, between us" (116). This merging of polarities is a metaphor for the multi-layeredness of the protagonist's identity. The fixation with memory admits a yearning for a time that existed before the disorienting effects of immigration. According to Alexandre Amprimoz and Sante Viselli, nostalgia represents a type of semiotic displacement.[7] When Nora goes to Italy to attend her husband's funeral, she becomes aware of the extent of her cultural anomie. The old village is as alien to her as the new world: "I don't really have a place anymore, I don't belong to any place" (125). Nostalgia is a defense against the insecurities of cultural emergence. It is, to paraphrase Antonino Mazza, a means of rejoining the anthropological memory to the self.[8] On an ironic level, nostalgia counters the protagonist's attempt to arrive at an essential self. Such sentimentality implies a kind of inadequacy, a longing for an idyllic past out of a sense of despair over a fractured present. This need for personal affirmation leads to the knowledge that both the old and new societies are inescapably complex, contradictory, and disjunctive. The act of remembrance heralds the discontinuities of history and culture, and highlights the fragmenting of the Italian Canadian subject.

4. *Lack of Closure*

The conclusion of *Made in Italy* underscores the discord and incertitude of ethnicity. Symbolism and imagery set up a kind of circular movement which connects the beginning and the conclusion of Nora's autobiography. In the opening scene, the transition from darkness to light parallels Nora's movement from a state of trepidation, of being unable to give meaning to her life, to an assertion of her individuality. In the conclusion of the text, the image of the sky smeared with dark smoke, which subtly mirrors the chiaroscuro world of the opening scene, foregrounds the failure of her quest for clarity: "I have sought in vain to explain to myself the reasons for the events which have occurred" (215). The present has been a monstrous repetition of a past which she has tried to transcend. The circularity and gloominess of the beginning and ending of the narrative transmit a sense of fatalism and suggest a form of closure. However, there is an ambiguity to the conclusion which prevents a finalization of meaning. Nora is enveloped in daylight, yet she has reembraced the darkness which surrounded her at the beginning. Darkness appears to be symbolic of tragedy in Canada. Darkness is linked to death, and hints at the expiration and transmutation of the old culture. The dead emblematize the cipher-like character of ethnicity in the new country: "the dead belong to themselves and the truth they have reached is impenetrable, incommunicable" (215-216). The act of submerging herself in a psychic underworld invests Nora with an inner power. This journey into the unconscious is Nora's attempt to reembody her peasant ancestry which now she sees as everlasting and indeterminate. The novel begins as it ends. Nora inhabits a world without clear frames of reference: "I have entered a dimension where time and space are unbounded"(2). The collapsing of history and culture educes the breakdown of cultural boundaries. The instabilities and transformations of new world ethnicity come to the fore. Such tumult and radical change are perceived to be nihilistic and "there is nothing left but the possibility of madness" (216). Indeterminacy interrupts the text's circular movement and prevents Nora's autobiography from coming to its natural fatal end.

5. *Death*

Death is an overarching trope in Italian Canadian writing. It often calls attention to the difficulties and tragic ironies of immigration. As Alexandre Amprimoz and Sandro Viselli observe, "There are many forms of death: perpetual marginalization, total assimilation, indifference or silence and invisibility."⁹ Nora as well as the other characters of this novel assume a variety of symbolic positions which enable them to cope with identity reformation. Italian Canadian literary texts render cultural loss as a sort of spiritual dissolution: "To abandon the language of your forefathers is to begin to die."¹⁰

The section on Vanni's death symbolically encapsulates the tension between ethnic identity and upward mobility. Tamara Palmer contends that this conflict threatens the immigrant's stability in the host country: "whether their quest focuses on the . . . spiritual goal of integrating disparate elements that constitute their lives, or the material goal of achieving wealth to prove their worthiness, [ethnic] protagonists . . . have few effective guides . . . the journey to either is tortuous, complicated by the . . . physical and social barriers that make it difficult for immigrants and their children to find a paradise in the New World."¹¹ While Moratti's obsessive hard work and economic success move him out of the working class, they diminish his already strained marriage and damage his health. Nora does not go back to Italy to celebrate her family's accomplishments in Toronto but to mourn the death of a Canadianized husband. This brings her to a desolate village: "My parents were dead. The abandoned house on the street had been sold by Michele, years before . . . The houses which were clustered together, on the road to the farm, still covered with pink and white plaster, now faded and with some additional cracks closer to the rooftops" (122-123). The subsequent deaths of her two sons, Andrea and Matteo, who have both scaled the class ladder, recapitulate the cost of abandoning the traditional culture and absorbing the values of mainstream society.

The incinerator spews smoke like a crematorium, a reminder of this novel's unrelenting preoccupation with the dying of the old culture. The dead embodied in the smoke do not symbolically meld into the sky, and join their ancestors, thus affirming cultural continuity. Instead, they descend on the city as ash and continue to haunt the living: "It [the smoke] falls on us in a fine dust; it attaches to our skin when we perspire; it penetrates our lungs when we breathe; it chokes us and causes us to wither" (215). The persistent allusions to decay and death tacitly acknowledge the passing of the traditional way of life. Elegy is used to signify the recuperation of the ancestral culture within the strictures of the host country. Beneath this elegiac mode lies a sentimental idealizing of the old world as a place of virtue and innocence. Ardizzi, nevertheless, subverts such idealization by depicting peasant society as precarious, onerous, and disunified. In this case elegy is contradictory: it signals the breaking down of traditional culture and confirms the appearance of a new and multiple identity. The sense of loss, implied by the use of elegy, affirms not just the power of old ways but also indirectly attests to a process of transformation.

6. *Chronology*

The chronological structure in *Made in Italy* embodies the many-sidedness of the protagonist. The first half of the novel intermingles the present and the past; Nora tries to give meaning to her life by navigating through a plethora of memories. The present tense makes her experiences immediate. It conjures up various states of being: wakefulness, dream, and memory. The use of the past tense (Nora's flashbacks) demonstrates the protagonist's distance from her own history. The new world refracts the inherent conflicts in the Moratti household. Urban society's stress on individuality weakens the fragile bonds between wife and husband, between parents and children. By juxtaposing events of the present to episodes from the past, Ardizzi punctuates the opposition that exists between two cultures. This confrontation will eventually lead to the gradual disintegration of the Moratti family. Through this stylistic device, Ardizzi is able to accentuate the division in her characters' attitudes and positions. Nora is unhesitantly censorious of the values of Italian as well as mainstream culture, even though she admits that they have framed her view of the world. Nonetheless it is the past that continues to direct the present; the smell of Matteo's body odour reminds Nora of the virility of her dead husband.

The first five chapters of the novel juxtapose the protagonist's current situation in Toronto to her life in the past. Flashbacks encompass her relationship with her adult children, key moments in the old country, and her marriage to Vanni/John in both Italy and Canada. Past events are "determining factors" (40) which shape the present. More importantly, Nora regards individuals as products of specific cultural contexts; she cannot "separate . . . people from their culture" (92). The overlayering of dream, memory, and experience, and of past and present time permits Ardizzi to put into question the historical accuracy of Nora's autobiography. The connections between past and present are often obscure. There is a lack of comprehensibility about what truly happened and how events have occurred. In fact, Ardizzi problematizes the autobiographical mode which traditionally assumes a unified subject. Identity formation is unclosed, intricate, and dynamic. The disruption of temporal linearity challenges the fixity of things and the ethnic subject suddenly becomes inconstant.

7. *Irony, Juxtaposition, and Old and New World Identities*

The juxtaposition of different story lines adds to "the experiential density of the literary text" and exposes the contradictory actions and attitudes of the mostly Italian-descended characters. Their cultural identities become "indeterminate [and] perhaps indeterminable."[12] Juxtaposition makes conspicuous the dissimilarities in gender roles in the Abruzzese-Italian immigrant family and in society at large. Interwoven stories generate a set of contrasting ironies which divulge the incoherence and instability of the ethnic and gendered subject. The second and third chapters, for example, link Nora's early years with Vanni to her granddaughter's involvement with Keith, an English Canadian. Nora's parents and brother disapprove of Vanni, believing him to be wanton and shiftless. This is similar to the scene in which Amelia berates Anna for her lack of judgement in wanting to marry a man who has no immediate economic prospects. In these two stories, both women rebel against their parents' suppositions of what constitutes an acceptable union, valorizing romantic love instead.

An ironic conjunction prevails between the protagonist's life and that of her granddaughter. Nora's and Vanni's lovemaking during their wedding night mixes eroticism with subtle inklings of male violence. In the ensuing episode, Anna visits Nora's house, where she proclaims her love for Keith. This scene is followed by young Nora's harrowing discovery that she has unwittingly substituted the harshness of marriage for the confinement of family. Nora's involuntary seclusion in her apartment is contrasted to Vanni's freedom of movement as a broker, his carousing and womanizing. Nora's sexual relationship with her husband is disturbingly ambiguous. Repression, abuse, and eroticism are closely intertwined: "He would come to me with an overpowering urgency to which I responded with a willingness I didn't want him to see" (61). Nora's subordination to male authority is reinforced by her mother's passivity and servitude, and by references to her brother's maltreatment of Emelia, his long-suffering fiancee. These flashbacks unstintingly portray the brutality of southern Italian patriarchy, and collide with the description of Anna's and Keith's harmonious and reciprocal relationship. In spite of Nora's doubts about the future of their union, the young lovers remain untouched by the self-destructiveness and violence which overwhelm the other couples in the novel. Anna, who has become integrated into urban society, and Keith, her English Canadian counterpart, represent the possibilities of a new world identity divested of the harmfulness of immigrant culture. The idealizing of the third generation Italian is blunted by the couple's naivete and by the implication that they are not immune to disillusionment and failure. While Nora supports her granddaughter's relationship with Keith, she suspects the break-up of their love since "life is not generous with anyone, and reality is its dark side" (54). The juxtaposition of Nora and Anna's separate narratives exploit the ironies and perspectival ambiguities of ethnicity which permeate the entire text.

The ironic juxtapositions of story lines persist in the fourth chapter. Young Nora's life in the old country is placed alongside her present situation in Canada. Nora compares the insularity and anonymity of urbanism to the intimacies of her hometown, a "noisy world without secrets [and] we entered [it] through windows and doors opened wide" (73). Unlike John, Nora has no emotional attachment to her well-to-do neighbourhood. Her husband's success has released her from the gender constraints of southern Italy. This irony is pinpointed in the juxtaposition of Nora's tiny living space in Italy to the luxuriousness of her Toronto house. Amelia's deprecation of Anna's relationship and her brothers' liaisons with non-Italian women is met with an inconsistent response from Nora. Even though she supports her granddaughter's decisions about her life, Nora fearfully acknowledges Amelia's assertion that both her sons, Andrea and Matteo, have discarded conventional familial values.

The protagonist's divergent viewpoints emanate from a complicated personality. Paradoxically, self-definition for Nora is predicated on individual freedom: it is sustained by an unfaltering dedication to family. Juxtaposed to this is young Nora's stay at her parents-in-law's farm during the war. The brief experience of emancipation from the bondage of matrimony foreshadows the protagonist's subsequent, albeit limited, independence as an immigrant woman. Nora's rancorous marriage exposes the gender oppressions of the old world and nourishes the ironies of ethnicity. The interminable vacillation between resistance and loyalty to the parochial culture stresses the indecisiveness of Nora's life.

Juxtaposition generates a remarkably ambivalent representation of Canadian society. Against Nora's initial romanticizing of the new world, one finds inserted a severe picture of physical and spiritual imprisonment which emblematizes her early experiences as an immigrant: "The cage in which we moved had become ever smaller, leaving only a hole for breathing" (93). The crammed living quarters in Toronto ("three little rooms on the second floor" with a "shared" bathroom (93)) seem to be an ironic reiteration of Nora and Vanni's sparsely furnished and constricted apartment in Italy. The orderliness of the Moratti dwelling in the old country, which Nora reconstitutes in their makeshift Toronto lodgings, is in diametrical opposition to the squalid living space of the owners of the boarding house. This unfavourable depiction of the Canadian family is magnified by the landlady's (Mrs. Turner) chronic alcoholism and appalling neglect of her children. For Nora, the subsequent purchase of a new home increases the drudgery of domestic work. The allusion to the grim architecture of the suburbs ("grey houses, cages for a crowded and invisible existence" (94)) further multiplies the image of incarceration.

Nora's autobiography articulates a deluded essentialist bifurcation in which the superficiality of the new world is positioned against the authenticity of the old. Ardizzi communicates Vanni's integration into capitalist society by referring to his impeccably polished demeanour and frenetic business practice. Assimilation for the immigrant is likewise represented in the images of Andrea in an elegant dark suit, complemented by a well-furnished and commodious office, and of Amelia luxuriating in her middle-class lifestyle. In contrast, Nora, immured in her home, carries on with the traditions and customs of her native culture. Countering the materialism, rationalism, and pretention of her assimilated children, Nora articulates images of simplicity and naturalness. She projects herself as being a person of "primitive, linear convictions" (150) who has "never separated from [her] origins" (147).

Through a series of arresting contradictions, the text destabilizes the cultural binaries of the protagonist's narrative. Nora effects her autonomy by working at a local factory and by constructing a feminine space in a commodious, suburban home. Her actions motivate her quarrel with the moral premises of urban-capitalist society. Nora's contradictory stance links her to her two sons, who are themselves an aggregate of interrelated and hostile viewpoints. The depiction of Andrea's and Matteo's wilful assimilation — their personal development through their intimacies with non-Italian women and economic betterment through professional activity — is counterpointed by the pathology of integration, by emotional and familial distress. The unravelling of the two brothers' complicated and conflicting value system reflects itself in their attraction towards their dangerous lovers, to whom they remain loyal out of a self-serving, yet culturally ingrained, sense of duty.

The ironic juxtaposition of the two cultures illuminates a world "of shifting perspectives" and an inexhaustible repertoire of "truth-options."[13] By mapping out the diverse socio-ideological structures imbedded in the protagonist's view of the world, juxtaposition argues against essentialist ethnicity. It buttresses the self-consciousness of the protagonist's narrative: prominently figured is a questioning and reconstructing of personal history and identity, a deliberate refurbishing of memories, and the rethinking of the immigrant experience and attendant cultural processes. Nora Moratti comments on the material forces which have shaped her life and admits that cultural systems are arbitrary. She constantly struggles against this knowledge by espousing a timeless and organic ethnic identity. The intersecting of conflicting and relative ideological suppositions prevents her from attaining a unified Italian Canadian subjectivity.

In the fifth chapter, Peggy's abhorrence of her husband Andrea's conventionality and lack of emotion is contrasted to Nora's self-reliance: "My role as mother and wife had . . . become meaningless . . . An unknown force attracted me to the outside world, toward . . . the city" (111). There is an ironic undertone to this contrast. Like Nora, Peggy once thought that the new world would be less burdensome than her homeland, Ireland, where she experienced poverty and sexual abuse. Peggy's disappointment with Andrea's traditionalism and materialism mirrors Nora's own fractious relationship with Vanni. The parallel between Peggy and Nora is strengthened when Ardizzi juxtaposes Nora's autonomy to her husband's death in the old country. Juxtaposition imparts the ironic reversal of Nora and Vanni's fortunes. Nora's ascent — her assertion of her individuality and her economic independence from John — coincides with his descent and unexpected death. John slowly loses control not only over Nora's life but his own. Nora ironically states: "I was hired in a factory which made women's clothes until John's death" (112). Her employment at a sweat-shop is doubly ironic since the novel implies that Nora passed from one form of servility to another. Nora's manual labour undoubtedly rises from the documented history of Italian immigrant women in Canada. Women, for the great part, were employed in the textile or other light-manufacture industries, and had to face many privations: they received poor pay, worked long shifts and in hazardous conditions.

Personal history, however, does not bring Nora closer to her daughter-in-law. Nora views Peggy as a cultural outsider. Peggy refuses to conform to the Italian value system, which acts as a barrier to self-actualization. Like Nora in her marriage to Vanni, Peggy refuses to define herself according to the stereotypical roles of women. The dramatic irony is enhanced by Nora's convoluted relations with her eldest son. Nora's denunciation of Andrea's obsessive materialism and maltreatment of his wife is negated by her cultural prejudices against Peggy. Nora admits earlier in the novel that she emotionally neglected her son when he was a child. The ironic suggestion here is that Andrea's disastrous relationship with Peggy is both the result of a poor family life and Nora's own turbulent marriage. Not only is Nora coldly imperious as Andrea in her need for self-control, she is also complicit in the suffering of others.

By juxtaposing Nora's and Jane's stories, Ardizzi expands the portrayal of Nora's duplicitous ethnic/gender identity. Jane is being terrorized by her estranged husband. Yet Nora is not sympathetic to her plight and does not see her as an ally in the fight against male domination. Disturbingly Nora considers her to be a threat to the equilibrium of the Moratti family. Despite the patriarchal nature of Italian Canadian culture, Matteo seems to offer Jane an environment which gives her more freedom than she had in her previous marriage. Jane's bond with Matteo ironically undercuts Nora's hold over her son. Although Nora describes Matteo and Jane's union as being "uncertain" (140), she is unwilling to accept the indeterminacy of her own existence or to acknowledge the unstated conflict between herself and her son. Nora's criticism of her sons' partners is contrasted to her empathy for Mrs. Turner, who is overwhelmed by domestic responsibilities and unrelieved poverty.

As this contrast suggests, Nora's class consciousness motivates her hostility towards Peggy and Jane, two middle-class women, and her support of Mrs. Turner, who is trapped by her working-class environment. The ironic juxtaposition of these markedly opposed attitudes discloses the multi-sidedness and contrariness of ethnicity in the new world.

Tragic events in chapter eight and nine enact the breakdown of the Italian Canadian family. Ardizzi contrasts Matteo's and Jane's murder, at the hands of her jealous husband, to the accidental and grisly death of Andrea and Peggy. This contrast marks the deadly opposition of cultural ideologies. Yet there are striking similarities between the two tragic events. Both take place at the Moratti cottage, the site of John's infidelities. The two juxtaposed scenes amplify the brutality of Nora's marriage to Vanni, and are full of contradiction and irony. In each, the male acts as the aggressor, engaged in lethal combat with a less powerful woman. As the scene with Andrea and Peggy indicates, the woman is depicted as being equally violent and destructive. This delineation of gender relations is concretized within a specific social framework. According to Nora, not only did Matteo and Andrea stray from traditional Italian culture, with its accepted allocation of gender roles and division of labour, they also chose non-Italian women as their partners. Although Nora attempts to balance her domestic and public lives, Jane and Peggy enact their autonomy by repudiating approved forms of dependent femininity. Matteo and Andrea's doubtful relationships are compared to that of Amelia and Riccardo, who, despite their meretricious display of wealth, are a conventional Italian couple. Of the three adult Moratti children, Amelia is the only one whose marriage remains intact in the novel.

8. *Female Space*

The representation of female space simultaneously embraces and usurps conventional assumptions about womanhood. The text employs a cluster of nature images which are related, alternately, to a feminine ideal and the dark side of sexuality.

In an essay on Vera Lysenko's *Yellow Boots*, which refers to *Made in Italy*, Beverely Rasporich states that "very often . . . the typical pattern of the female *Bildungsroman*, identified as that of a deadlocked dialectical series of encounters with the matrilinear world of nature and the patrilinear social structure, is assuaged with a . . . positive association of woman and nature."[14] Allusions to Nora being spiritually transported by nature pervade the narratives of the old and new world.

Several images of women in nature personify the nurturing potentialities of the feminine freed from the structures of patriarchy. Young Nora is spellbound by the surrounding landscape of the Moratti farm. The figure of her mother sits in the family garden which is encompassed by "the orchard . . . the fields of the plain . . . and the river in the horizon" (23) Nora valorizes the old world by eliciting the physicality of southern rural Italians and their intimate connection to the land: "We . . . carry the imprint of the earth" (7). Her "roughness" and "blunt ways" are embodiments of the rocky and "barren" (15) terrain of her village in the Gran Sasso. ("Gran Sasso" literally means big stone). The text emphasizes Italian femininity by linking the "thick . . . smell of wild flowers" (81) along the mountainscape to "the tepid perfume of the earth" (72) in the Toronto suburbs.

This idyllic imagery is contrasted to Gran Sasso's economic and cultural depravation and to the wasting away of individual ability: "There was . . . the director of the post office . . . artistically inclined, impoverished by the region that had denied him any possibility of furthering himself" (22). Nora likens the traditions of her village to "musty" (23) walls which are "erected as barriers before our destinies" (23). Enclosure reappears throughout Nora's recollections of the past. She sees her early life circumscribed by the "small space" of the village "whose limits were church and fountain" (23). Contemplating the fate that awaits her as wife and mother, she senses that "the world ha[s] . . . closed before me and ha[s] shrunk within the confines of the hills" (26). Communal activity and celebration are undercut by economic misery: "the religious atmosphere . . . had nothing religious about it, except for the resignation and the poverty [of the worshippers]" (44). This ambience is reproduced in the detailing of Nora and Vanni's near-indigence in the local town. Such bleak memories of the old country are juxtaposed to the story of Nora's return journey. Not only has Gran Sasso been altered by time, but it also has become strange and unwelcoming. Immigration has severed her ties to the old world: "the thread that bound me to these places has been broken" (125). Her identity is shattered: "I found shreds of myself little by little as I neared my homeland" (122). Despite this, Nora acknowledges the ineradicability of her cultural roots. She wants to fuse "earth and flesh" (126) and reclaim an essential Italian femininity.

Imagery associated with the natural environment embodies the enmities of gender relations and is invested with paradox and ambiguity. Organic femininity is transmitted through the seasonal cycles, the omnipresence of sky and trees, sweet-scented flowers in bloom, and the lushness of a vegetable garden in Canada. This is opposed to the bald aggressiveness of the male subject who continually violates the sanctity of the natural environment. Repulsed by rural life and unaffected by the beauty of the Italian countryside, Vanni disrupts his wife's tranquil stay with her in-laws. Vanni is described by his commercial exploitation of farmland in Canada and his many infidelities at Wasaga Beach. Nora's narrative also implies that males harness the lethal powers of nature. With "eyes filled with a turbulent glow" (175), Peter issues malevolently from the woods and heartlessly shoots Jane and Matteo. Contact with nature releases Andrea's animalism: "His thick, strong body, covered with dense, dark hair, stands out in the rectangle of the door with a savage, male imperiousness" (206). This startling image precedes his vicious rape of his wife, and is contrasted to a later description of Peggy, who is traumatized by her rape, as she wanders inside a thicket of woods "like a snared beast" (208).

Nature is the terrain of female violence, whether intentional, as in the case of Peggy's retaliation against Andrea which leads to both their deaths, or unintentional, as in the scene when Matteo is engulfed by Jane's calamitous history with her husband. This harmful side of femininity is repeated in Nora's animosity towards Vanni and by Amelia's habitual nagging of Riccardo. Coerciveness and self-destruction are qualities which cross gender lines. This view is advanced by joining the primality of nature — "the branches, deep into the earth and between the entangled bushes" (207) — to the irrationality of the characters, who are overtaken by "secret entangled and invisible forces [which] regurgitate in each of us" (209). Heightening the horrific scenes at the cottage is a tenebrous, cruel, and remote nature: "the sky looks on with indifference at the storms which are unleashed down here" (214). Allusion to the sky enlarges the text's symbolic use of nature imagery. At the start of the novel, there is a bright and limitless sky, a *tabula rasa*, which is suggestive of hope and creativity. This is pitted against the concluding image of the garbage incinerator spewing its white smoke of despair and the end of possibility. Sinister allusions to nature inject a gothicism into Nora's narrative as she descends into a nightmarish world. This landscape in chaos finds a correspondence in the madness of fatal violence and in Nora's mental breakdown at the end of the novel.

Beverly Rasporich argues that "madness . . . is less a psychological exploration than the social statement that it is difficult for [an ethnic] woman to develop her full potential and . . . identity in the acceptable social role of marriage . . . it is quite predictable that she will be disordered, unnatural, crazy in her entrapment."[15] The motif of madness personifies the dilemmas and tentativeness of ethnicity and femininity in the new world: "Uprooting, resettling, cultural dichotomy, divided loyalties, self-hate and self-doubt," notes Helen Barolini, are tied to "the problems between generations, the problems between the sexes as men and women search for new roles."[16] Irony, uncertainty, and contradiction counteract the gender binaries of Nora's autobiography.

Variegated images of domesticity uncover the disjunction of the gendered subject. The home is the site of patriarchal oppression, but it is also associated with a woman's economic and social role. Although young Nora fails to escape domestic serfdom when she leaves her family and marries Vanni, she is able to construct an environment which shields her from the brutishness of her husband and which nurtures her children.

The protagonist-narrator treats domesticity as the locus of traditional Italian femininity through a female community. Three generations of women — grandmother, aunt, and daughter-in-law — manage collaboratively the farm and the extended family, while the male figure, the grandfather, is dependent on them for his care. The evocation of a female community combines with the rendering of Nora's feminine identity in Canada. Despite the hardships of immigration, demonstrated by the Morattis' poor accommodations in Toronto, and the landlady's dereliction of her maternal duties, the protagonist provides for her children and acts as a surrogate mother for the Turner siblings. She sees in Mrs. Turner's plight an image of her own subjugation. Predictably, it is Nora who humanizes the family's newly-built, ostentatious suburban home. In contrast, Vanni and Andrea transgress domestic integrity by sexually assaulting their wives. Often the two men treat their home as a place to recuperate in or as a mere material possession. Ardizzi's representation of domestic space summons up negative images of female presence. Wanting to maintain her influence, Nora almost chains Matteo psychologically to the home. Amelia's complete control over the household is a means to dominate her husband. Peggy attacks Andrea's self-esteem by carrying out an adulterous affair in their home.

This countervailing imagery undermines the narrator's indictment of patriarchy and identifies the domestic pathology of the Italian Canadian. The recurrent image of Nora seated by the front window of her domicile and looking out detachedly at a sprawling cityscape suggests a state of exile. In the opening scene, an elderly woman breaks the darkness by letting the daylight into her home. This beginning is tied to the conclusion in which a paralytic Nora watches the funereal dance of seagulls as smoke streaks the arc of the sky. Domesticity shelters the protagonist from the perceived insecurities and dangers of urbanism, but it also swallows her, reducing her to a despondent and static figure.

Alongside this contradiction, there looms a picture of modernity, of fleeting time and impermanence. In this urban setting, everyone is constantly in motion, continually migrating from place to place. The hyperactivity of capitalist-consumer society is captured in the cars rushing by at dizzying speed. Viewing the coming and going of different cultural groups in her neighbourhood, Nora claims that "houses [are] a transit stop, never a destination" (73). This social instability supports the notion that Canada historically has been a country of immigrants.

As a polyvalent trope, ethnicity signals both the fluidity of modern life — "we are all immigrants even if we remain fixed in our own world, among our own people" (16) — and the indefiniteness of the Italian immigrant: "you will remain a wave without a shore/ you will never know that the whole wide world is/your home" (xv). Uncertainty, discontinuity, and the decentring of the ethnic subject underlie the ironic portrayal of place and people in *Made in Italy*.

6
The Social Construction of Subjectivity in *The Lion's Mouth*

Caterina Edwards' novel, *The Lion's Mouth*, depicts immigration and the process of adjustment from the perspective of the daughter of immigrant parents. The protagonist-narrator, Bianca Bolcato, is able to enter mainstream society, despite its intolerance of cultural difference, in a more productive manner than Nora Moratti in *Made in Italy*. The experience of reaching adulthood in Edmonton and her questioning of the gender role assumptions of Canadian and Venetian society alleviate her cultural marginalization. While gender is an important component of her identity formation, Bianca implies that underlying social processes and not just patriarchy itself shape the attitudes of men and women and their relations to each other. Instead of an antagonistic view of Italian and Canadian culture, the protagonist believes that both men and women constantly invent and reinvent their gender roles to meet societal expectations. In doing so, men and women become captive to the very ideas and behaviour that they no longer deem acceptable. An individual is not simply the product of external forces. Through personal choice, however limited it may be, one can have a measure of control over his/her life. This sensibility is in marked contrast to Nora Moratti's sense of resignation as an immigrant woman in a male-based ethnic family.

In *The Lion's Mouth*, ethnicity is made up of many subject-positions which are attached to a varied, arbitrary, and frequently discrepant grouping of culturally-based beliefs and attitudes. This indeterminacy is represented through the employment of various formal techniques which destabilize the possibility of closure. The reflexivity of storytelling, in which the protagonist-narrator provides a commentary on the production of her text, broadcasts in part the conscious and incessant invention and reinvention of ethnicity and femininity. The rewriting of the past, of stories about life in the old country, and about immigration and adjustment in the new society, serves a curative purpose.[1]

Juxtaposition, such as the continual intercutting between Bianca's and Marco's story, highlights the ambiguities and multi-layeredness of the protagonist's subjectivity as she moves back and forth between two divergent and elaborate cultural contexts. Remembrance, infused with a nostalgic/elegiac tone, exposes the discontinuities of history and subverts the essentializing of ethnicity. The social construction of cultural and gender identities, an important part of this novel, is communicated through the leitmotif of performance, role-playing, masking and unmasking, and the act of artifice-making. References to social history, such as immigration and political unrest in Venice, suggest that ethnicity derives from specific, conflicting, and always-changing material conditions. Underlying these formal techniques is the ironic mode, which subtly profiles the unending inconsistencies and complexities of identity formation.

1. *Reflexivity and Storytelling*

By composing her autobiography and in recreating the life of her cousin in Venice, Bianca examines the suppositions of two opposed cultures and reveals to the reader the contingencies and disjunctions of ethnicity. In the process of writing her double narrative, Bianca presents past versions of these two stories. In each version, the protagonist comments directly on the production of her work, constantly providing extra-textual information and the motivations for her writing. Her writing is influenced by external and contentious forces which prevent a congruous depiction of lived experience. Italian Canadian identity is represented as something that is socially produced, continually changing shape and perspective as it shifts in and out of personal, social, and historical contexts. The multi-texturedness, stylization, and symbolic nature of the Venetian story further imply that identity is contrived and imagined.

The narrator-character borrows from a variety of literary genres — romance, melodrama, espionage — and treats characterization, imagery, symbolism, and atmosphere as a means of conveying states of mind and cultural viewpoints. This conscious literariness contests the sort of writing that relies on the reconstruction of personal and social histories. It counters the supposedly epistemological aim of the storytelling: "I want to be the one who not only knows but illuminates the truth."[2] All the characters in this novel, at times even the protagonist-narrator herself, are presented as figures of the imagination. The reflexivity of the novel, evident in Bianca Bolcato's self-consciousness in telling her story and in the literariness of her Venetian narrative, emphasizes the constructedness and indeterminacy of the ethnic subject.

Each attempt to assemble the two narratives is contradictory and uncertain. In the first version, at the age of fifteen, Bianca fashions a sombre picture of a lonely and isolated Italian immigrant girl. Her cousin, "who represented Venice lost" (75), inspires memories of a beloved country but ultimately fails to save "the doomed heroine" from her predicament. The protagonist-narrator tries to simplify the meaning of the story, and remarks that it "illuminates the depth of the shock my family's emigration from Venice to Canada caused" (76). Its underlying ambivalence refutes such a view. The inconsistent depiction of the Venetian cousin conveys a strong urge to return home and foreshadows her disillusionment with Venetian culture. Cultural transmutation issues in a conflicting portrayal of the old world.

In the second version, heroic images of Marco Bolcato are corroded by hints of moral turpitude and by allusions to deception and betrayal: "she was seduced and abandoned by the European, set on the path of her destruction" (108). The teen-aged Bianca still resists assimilation even as she spurns what she considers to be her parents' ossified ways. Sidelined by both cultures, Bianca invents a multicultural character who unites her North American and European identities: "She was a Joan Baez look alike, travelling in Europe. Her main characteristic . . . was her innocence" (108).

The third version magnifies the paradoxical nature of ethnicity by overlayering contrasting images of the two cultures. The story of a woman who sees the shortcomings of her Venetian heritage as she builds a home for herself in the Canadian West is juxtaposed against inferences of a socially intolerant and largely unformed new society. Again, Marco is an embodiment of this complicated rendering of the process of identity formation in the new world: "So although you were made to represent the flaw . . . you did not carry all the blame" (144). Integration into the host country, which, in Bianca's early twenties, occurs through choice and the force of circumstance, produces a mixed identity. Although this multiplicity is figured in the image of a heroine who is "a Canadian girl with a Venetian background" (144), the key referent is the old world. The excesses of Bianca's Venetian fantasy indicate the extent of her discomfiture with the insularity of immigrant culture and the unimaginativeness of a Western Canadian lifestyle: "I gave my heroine wondrous acid trips through the history of Venice . . . I also gave her . . . lovingly detailed sex scenes. 'Gianni' and 'Serena' were lusty and inventive, coupling in unusual places and positions" (144).

The hedonistic solipsism of the central character mirrors Bianca's fierce craving for a time before cultural transformation. It ironically intimates an anxiety-ridden feminine sexuality which transposes images from North American popular culture onto scenes from Italian photo-romances. At the same time, it suggests the sensuality and decadence of the old world. The ancient city is an overdetermined trope for it signifies the intensity of Italianness, the unrecoverability of a lost identity, the primality of human appetites, and the onset of social decay. This third version of Bianca's novel is likewise disjunctive in its representation of Canada as a place which culturally marginalizes the protagonist yet cushions her against the stress of living in a traditional Italian household and releases her creative energy. The narrative studiously eschews a binary opposition of cultures and exploits the ambiguity of conflicting tendencies.

The paradoxes which suffuse all three stories inform the problematic of ethnicity and underline Bianca Bolcato's conscious and habitual reframing of her identity. As she herself acknowledges, ethnicity is challengingly intricate and infinitely variable: "downfalls, no matter what the kind, were complex, difficult" (144).

The self-reflexivity of the storytelling is strengthened by the use of distancing devices and an interventionist narrator. The didacticism of the protagonist nullifies the dramatic tension of the narrative. She revisits events from the past to advance specific viewpoints that she maintains in the present. The story of her relationship with Jack turns into a social commentary on male and female conditioning; the inadequacy of gender roles results in the decision to leave her boyfriend. The protagonist's intercession lacks sentimentality and is an attempt to guide the reader as the scene unfolds in past time. This distancing technique recurs throughout the text. It happens when her parents refuse to give up archaic traditions and embrace modern Italian values: "They would not acknowledge that habits and guidelines could have changed in Italy since their youth. They clung to 'their way,' but disconnected from the society it expressed" (108). Bianca addresses the reader who is ostensibly her cousin. Beneath the specific "you" is the implied reader of the text. Expectations of a realist narrative often purposely are left unfulfilled, so that the reader, like Bianca, can critically assess the issues that are being presented. The narrator's interventions reflect her self-estrangement; although she describes emotions and details from the past, she moves outside of them, as if she is scrutinizing the behaviour of someone else.

Reflexiveness prevents narrative closure. Both stories which the protagonist now presents to the reader indicate another permutation of identity. As Francesco Loriggio observes: "When [Bianca] finishes the new draft we cannot know whether she has been faithful to [Marco] or whether she has once more arranged his life to suit her present state of mind, as she did on previous occasions."[3] Each subsequent version of her story-within-a-story is a narrative in-process, and invalidates the previous one as an approximation of the truth, since it delineates a radicalizing of perspective. The changeability of experience challenges the communicatory function of language, evident in the statement that "words . . . are things to be wrestled with, to be forced into the proper order" (48).

The problem with language is symptomatic of the difficulty of defining oneself in a volatile, culturally multi-tiered, and conflicted social environment. *The Lion's Mouth* implies that it is not just the linguistic difference between Bianca and Marco which causes estrangement but also the divergence of viewpoints. Storytelling is about the manufacturing of reality from the perspective of the writer: "I look out through your eyes. I become you. I make the story, the book" (180).

Fictiveness and a concomitant interpretive elasticity forestall narrational closure: "With me, it is always stories. And in the end it is all I can offer you" (180). The diverse characterizations of the Italian cousin repeats the contradictory action of the ethnic subject as she self-consciously reappropriates and rejects parts of her Italian heritage.

In her imagination, a sensitive and creative Marco energetically embraces the care-free lifestyle of Venice: "the city was the ancient way . . . the enjoyment that lay in the expanses of unfettered time" (148). The romanticizing of the ancestral culture is subsumed by a cynical and severely depressed individual who is divorced from the world around him. Cultural absence and the randomness of social contact underlie this inconsistent characterization of the Venetian: "I lay out a photo snapped by a sidewalk cameraman . . . we seem two strangers, caught in the frame by chance" (120).

Bianca Bolcato's narrative of Western Canada is equally disjunctive and provisional. Arrival in the host country is emotionally and psychologically disabling even "though I was with Mamma and Papa, I felt stripped of family, of friends, of familiar walls and buildings . . . I was exposed, alone in the nothingness" (77). Compared to the refulgent Venetian landscape, the prairies are monotonous and "desolate" (76), especially in the interminable winter months.

Acculturation, however, proves to be exceedingly contradictory and discordant. While Bianca eloquently elevates the enormous potential of the new society, she is often on her guard. She thinks that the new world is inclined to place utilitarianism and materialism above human values. Anticipating the unproductive use of government funds at the inauguration of a constructed waterfall, she quickly pushes her reservations aside. The beauty of the waterfall's design and motion recall the fleeting images of "the [fabled] watery city" (179).

Edmonton is perceived simultaneously as orderly, innovative, and "precarious, even transitory, an imposition rather than a natural growth" (47). It is an island in an oceanic sweep of prairie, economically and socially impermanent: "So many are here to take what they can. When the boom slackens . . . they will pack up their buildings and move on to a new camp" (47). The amassing of quick profits implies that community-building is not just doubtful but ultimately illusory. Industrial capitalism mercilessly exploits and constantly endangers the natural environment.

Bianca's paean to the wilderness is undermined by a nature that is totally circumscribed and visibly altered by technological-urban society: "even though . . . I can hear the roar of trucks on the nearby thoroughfare and almost smell the noxious fumes, in a minute I can lose myself to the ravine woods . . . [to] the . . . sound . . . of the running water and of the birds and squirrels in the trees, where only the smell is the scent of pine in wildflowers" (47). Disillusioned with modern Venetian society, the protagonist links Western Canada to the pioneering spirit of her ancient ancestors: "through their industriousness and will created joy from a barren marsh" (179). The amalgamation of cultures — the shaping of "vast spaces" and the learning of "the habit of art" (179) — inspire an idealization of the host country. From the materials of European culture, immigrants constitute a new and incorruptible community and identity. The new world, like the old, however, is an imaginative construct. It exists only as a projection of what the protagonist considers to be possible.

Storytelling works against the forming of a coherent identity. It unwittingly enacts the tensions and complexities of the

Italian Canadian subject. The protagonist as a writer expresses her attachment to the new land. Ensconced in her room, she isolates herself from the community that surrounds her. Ethnicity is highly mutable, open-ended, and yet to be realized imaginatively: "Canada, out there . . . this terrain, is also here, in us, uncreated, evolving."[4] Conventional storytelling orders disparate details into a comprehensible whole. It cannot, though, overcome linguistic and cultural differences: "I cannot write it in Italian, and you do not read English. I will never touch you at all" (180). The instabilities of traversing two opposed cultural fields are apparent in the continual revising of Marco's story: "As I look over those three earlier novels, I see that my changing needs, my shifting perceptions and understanding, cast you in different forms" (46).

Immigration challenges the fixity of cultural systems. Venice is amorphous, usually shrouded in ambiguity: "never this direct, cheerful shine but always a reflection flickering up from the canal" (46). The new world is as ephemeral and tenuous as the old and Edmonton "seems precarious, even transitory" (47).

2. *Juxtaposition*

The juxtaposing of two stylistically different narratives (Bianca and her cousin) seems to inscribe an opposed set of cultural relations. The disorienting effect of this juxtaposition mirrors "the shock" of "emigration" (76). The protagonist's "life was split into two seemingly inimical halves" (76). First person narration made immediate by its didacticism and self-reflexiveness transmits the protagonist's commitment to the redefining of identity in Canada. In Marco's story, the distancing effect of omniscient narration is bolstered by the use of irony. Omniscience facilitates a critical stance, and underlines the alterity of the Venetian subject. The ironizing of the characters' sociopolitical positions exposes a network of complicity and deception. While Marco is repelled by the vulgar commercialism of his employer, his complacent middle class life is dissociated from the harshness of socioeconomic realities. Elena's revolutionary activity is motivated as much by the need to fashion a new identity after the collapse of her childhood dreams as it is by her concern for the plight of the powerless. This political posturing opposes itself to Bianca's social commentary. Her aim is to expose the shortcomings of both Italian and Canadian culture and to posit an alternative and progressive way of life. References to history, culture, and politics confirm the relativity and moral turpitude of Venetian society.

Present time and the lack of a consistent chronology in Bianca's autobiography invokes the urgency, dynamism, and open-endedness of identity formation. In contrast, Marco's story transpires in past tense with a more linear sequencing of events and is interspersed with flashbacks. The narrative lasts a short time. It commences on Friday afternoon and ends on Sunday night. This short period of time lends an intensity to Marco's state of crisis. Unlike the protagonist's story, an identity in process, Marco's narrative depicts a life that has already run its course. Recurrent flashbacks usually conjure up images of a traumatic past: the bombing of the city during the Second World War, or the breakdown of Marco's marriage to Paola. This imagery suggests a society without hope or a future. The present tense in Bianca's autobiography hints at fluidity and possibility, while past time in the Venetian narrative underscores personal and collective stagnation. The use of montage and the continuous intercutting between two narrative movements give us a glimpse of the different sensibilities which have formed the two characters' identities.

Another technique is the jarring juxtaposition of literary genres. Autobiography, characterized by a measured self-reflection, clashes with a spy story which veers towards psychodrama. The thematic pattern of the Venetian narrative includes sexual and political subterfuge, adultery, betrayal, and eventual breakdown. This is a world of moral ambiguity and shifting allegiances. Elements of the pot-boiler systematically embody the frayed mental state of the protagonist, Marco Bolcato. There is a feeling of constant menace, the use of character-types (a femme fatale and an unsuspecting hero), the use of an expressionistic setting, evocative of claustrophobia and decay, and the depiction of psychological and physical violence. The

Venetian narrative is like a morality play. After satiating his sexual appetite in the arms of a manipulative ex-lover, the central character confesses his sins and accepts punishment through self-immolation. Moral clarity is subverted when Marco's consciousness (presented in the third person) melds with the voice of the assassin. Victim and victimizer become part of the same subjectivity.

The stylistic thrust of the text tilts against narratological separateness and the opposition of cultural identities. Bianca's brief appearances in the story she is telling — an adolescent who is infatuated with her charming but weary cousin — means that she too is a character-type. This recourse to self-fictionalization problematizes the historical credibility of her autobiography. In the text, the protagonist is a literary construct, not just a mimetic representation of a particular subjectivity.

The conscious fictionalization of one weekend in Marco's life borrows from the spy genre. It blurs the boundaries between biography and artifice-making. The two stories collapse into themselves and become figments of the protagonist's imagination. Bianca blends her subjectivity with that of her cousin. She inserts herself inside his head, so that he speaks through her. The compression and contraction of time are such that the first person narration spans almost an entire life, while the story of Marco unfolds over a two-day period. This compression coupled with the use of the present tense for the narrator's story and the past tense for Marco's counteracts the text's normal shift to linearity and cohesiveness.

The double narrative is an index of the conflict and plurality of living at the nexus of contending cultural discourses. The two cultural identities of the protagonist constantly interact, but they remain contiguous, always resisting unification. There is no essentialist Italian consciousness since it is perpetually altered by changing social forces. Venetian culture is overlayered with a largely symbolic Renaissance heritage as it ignites under the pressure of competing interests. Sentimentality verges on delusion and an inbred self-destructiveness partly activated by guilt characterizes the text's representation of Marco Bolcato as a modern Venetian.

In Canada, imported modes of behaviour ensure the survival of the immigrant. The exigencies of adjustment modify elements of the original culture. Italian Canadian identity must be negotiated through a set of obstacles, whether it is the mainstream's cultural intolerance — "The worst transgression of all was my writing of Italy" (152) — or the limitations of a patriarchal-matrifocal family. Losses and gains produce anxiety, self-doubt, and precarious cultural allegiances. Italianness is a provisional gesture. It allows the protagonist to proclaim her ethnicity; it is profoundly unfixed and multifarious.

3. Memory

Historical realities impede the recuperation of a singular identity through the enactment of memory. Memory is not coherent, continuous or seamless, but a sliding scale of contradictions and indeterminacies: "Venice, stone and water, Venice bride of the sea, bride of my dreams; she is the recurring motif that I cannot escape and I cannot capture" (175). Bianca believes that European civilization can avoid the ravages of the past by becoming part of a new society that is not constrained by history. In contrast, Marco Bolcato is haunted by horrific scenes from the past; he succumbs to the nihilism of history, and confirms that there is no present or future, only an endless repetition of dead time. This binarism, between the lack of history in the new and the long and tragic history of the old, is undermined by allusions in the Venetian narrative to inner, inexplicable forces which transcend history. The binarism is further subverted by the historicizing of Canada as a product of European presence, by the adoption of old world ingenuity and cultural patterns.

The text, moreover, insinuates that capitalist enterprise based on resource extraction has had a strong negative impact on the historical and social development of Alberta. The new moment is itself caught between two shifting cultural frameworks. They affect one another and resist homogenization. The "I" and the "Other" represent the interacting but differentiated cultural perspectives of the protagonist. Such diversity undermines the essentializing project of memory. It also ushers the reader into an irreducible and unrecoverable cultural history.

Memory ostensibly heralds the end of one historical period and the beginning of another. Bianca's early days in Venice and her subsequent return visits after she emigrates to Canada is set against a dynamic, colourful, and creative culture. Recollections of boisterous and energetic crowds during the summertime in the city with its endless canals, shops, and squares sentimentalize the past. Bianca slowly becomes assimilated. She delineates the dark side of modern Venetian society, emphasizing the connection between its current problems and a decadent and often oppressive history. Haunted by guilt, shame, and self-loathing, Marco is surrounded by a morally questionable social order which supplants the memories of a young, jubilant, and idealistic man. Memory summons up a time before innocence was lost — before personal, cultural, and spiritual disintegration. Memory anticipates the demise of the old way of life and signals the protagonist's growing allegiance to the host country.

The elegizing of the old world is contradictory. Ethnicity entails the reappropriation of the original identity at the same instant that Canadianness is being embraced. Ethnic subjectivity is not dichotomous and fixed but multiple and changeable. It encompasses past, present, and differing versions of its immigrant side while perpetually reforming itself in a complex and heterogeneous Canadian society. Remembrance is highly unstable; it is part of a field of experience that is contradictory and provisional.

4. *Role-playing*

Bianca continually assumes, deconstructs, and reconstructs her adverse and interlocking cultural identities: "Old masks replaced by new? The vision of the outsider, Italian, American, or [Western] Canadian, superseded by that of the native?"(48) The natural landscape, indefinable and mutable, complements the performance of newly acquired social roles: "the emotional slide . . . that coloured the country oppressive and infinitely barren, flipped up and back to be stored; a new one that painted the land familiar and supporting clicked into place" (48).

Role-playing, however, is often shaped by forces outside of Bianca's control. The cultural homogeneity of the educational system, from public school to university, makes Bianca the focus of cultural discrimination: "the circle [was] closing around me . . . 'We don't want DP's'"(78). Homogeneity tends to relegate her to the margins of social activity. Assimilative pressures result in the conscious appropriation of new self-images and viewpoints, evident in Bianca's longing "for ski jackets, jeans, shiny plastic shoes like everyone else's" (79). Appreciation of nature invigorates Bianca and gives her a sense of solace and peace. The reading of popular literature inspires romantic fantasies and advances a cultural perspective that is at odds with the seeming banality of her ethnic household. Bianca scrutinizes her parents from the outside, and questions their single-minded pursuit of economic stability. Ironically, the valorizing of a bourgeois English Canadianness — as is the case with Jody and her family's refinement, liberalism, and wealth — unwittingly signals Bianca's own preoccupation with upward mobility. Canadian identity is formed as much by reacting against the belief system of Italian culture as it is by adapting to the social structures of the mainstream. Underneath Bianca's hostility to her ethnicity and her parents is the suggestion that only by moving out of the immigrant enclave and attaining a university degree, which she finances without family help, can she improve her social standing.

Mainstream society is inaccessible in part because it is colonized and fragmented: "[My country] was hidden, obscured. The history, the literature I was taught was English or American. The TV, the movies, the model for life was strictly American" (146). It is also inaccessible because ethnicity is multiple and diffused, and, therefore, is unable to position itself securely within any specific cultural context. Bianca insists that she cannot animate her Italian traits, cannot "loosen the jaw. My mouth [cannot] open wide enough to let the words properly roll" (85), because "the Canadian style . . .

had been coded into my body and could not be unlearned" (85).

"Canadianness" is not a mere contrivance, "the mask" (84) which is superimposed on her Italian self. It is a constituent part of her subjectivity. Venetian attitudes are socially constructed; they still influence the protagonist's perceptions of herself. Bianca identifies her physical appearance with that of the women in Longhi's paintings, even though she realizes that such images are idealizations of a particular kind of Italian femininity.

The collision of intercultural perspectives produces an unstable and inconsistent ethnic subject. Immigration, assimilation, and ethnicization involve the appropriation, jettisoning, reappropriation, and reinvention of cultural identities. Italianness is separate from and coexists with Canadianness.

As the protagonist's narrative indicates, ethnicity locates itself in several conflicting social orders at once. Bianca professes that she has harmonized her warring identities; she acknowledges the cleavage between herself and Marco. The transgression of cultural boundaries generates a restive, self-conscious, and complex identity. The self-consciousness of the ethnic subject is communicated through the leitmotif of performance, the continual act of masking and unmasking.

The identities of the Italian characters are not represented as natural, static, or universal. Behaviour and outlook are affected by historically-specific and ever-changing social relations. In the Venice narrative, the mask signifies the arbitrary construction of assigned roles and is signalled by *Carnevale*. This age-old festivity, wherein people don various masks and costumes, legitimates the discarding of prescribed roles, the removal of social and class barriers, and the open expression of desire. "Carnival celebrated temporary liberation from the prevailing truth and from the established order," argues Mikhail Bakhtin, "it marked the suspension of all hierarchical rank, privileges, norms, and prohibitions."[5] During the merrymaking, Marco Bolcato is surrounded by a sea of masks, by shifting and unplaceable identities: "He knew them and did not know them . . . [their physical appearance] seemed random details rather than identifiable characteristics" (89).

The mask as an overdetermined sign makes obvious the deception and impermanence of culturally-created identities. The central character is repeatedly invested with theatrical characteristics. Not only is role-playing uncertain, for "no matter what mask he chose for himself, other saw him only in subordinate roles" (66), but it is also improvisational: "he felt as if he had stumbled upon a stage . . . Both he and [the audience] were waiting for the action to begin" (37). The execution of his spousal role is both steadying and disorienting: "[His wife] was part of him and yet not part . . . she seemed utterly strange, utterly alien to his flesh" (154). Self-images transmit the absurdity and grotesqueness of a socially imposed identity: "His own face in the mirror was ridiculous; bulbous nose, sunken cheeks — a comedy mask, worse, a gargoyle" (140). Other people deliberately act out their designated part, such as when his supervisor, Raponi, begins "to play the role for which he had been cast" (17).

Theatrical masks evoke the banality and one-dimensionality of facial features: "Marco . . . had the feeling he was facing not two human faces but the . . . masks of comedy and tragedy" (18). Role-playing turns people into functions: the medical doctors, the masked men, treat Marco's ill son with detachment. The enigmatic Elena personifies the factitiousness of public personas: she appears to him alternately as a cheap, worn-out, and sinister imitation of a sexpot, and as a sensual and breathtaking woman.

Powerful external conditions negate the development of an integrated personality. History is not continuous but disjunctive and destabilizing. This is exemplified in the ways that the brutality and horror of World War II have restructured Marco's identity. By internalizing his physical and psychic pain, evident in his dark thoughts, self-hate, and guilt, Marco compulsively reenacts his victimization: "he must finish his role, he must make his denunciation" (171). His face acquires the mask-like aspect of the lion, "*Bocca di leone,* the stretched mouth in agony without end" (172). The theatricality of the image confirms the performance-based nature of cultural identity.

Venice is the site of contending social, historical and material forces. Since the city's inception, its inhabitants have been engaged in an endless combat with the elements: "Unceasing work, unceasing struggle, were essential in shoring up the 'frail barrier' . . . against the claims of the sea" (93). The ancient city was once a splendid and culturally sophisticated place, emblematic of the achievement of European civilization: "Two thousand years of history: Greek, Byzantine, Gothic, Baroque, coexisting in harmonious balance, a melody of man's potential" (104). It now is threatened by the deadly onslaught of commerce and industry. Ancient structures are levelled to make way for commercial enterprise, such as "a new resort complex on the Lido" (16). The gradual deterioration of irreplaceable architecture demonstrates the insidious effects of pollution. Political corruption and instability, subversive activity, sporadic bombings aimed at civilians, and politically-motivated assassinations have turned the city into a war zone. Underlining this decline are references to historical moments, primarily the Renaissance and World War II, which are suffused with images of oppression and extreme violence. Yet Venice perseveres, continues to honour its traditions, continues in its indomitable manner to find creative solutions to difficult problems while cultivating a finely-textured lifestyle.

Social and historical discontinuity is communicated through a series of contradictory and indeterminate images. Venice is composed of shimmering surfaces, false fronts, stunning architectural facades and unspeakable and horrible realities: "[the] palace . . . appeared ethereal, a pink and white fantasy. How well it masked the inner warren of rooms and dungeons that was once the city's core of power" (15). The literariness of Venice as a place of stone and water alludes to John Ruskin's study of the fabled city, and emphasizes its artifice-making quality. The ancient citadel, anthropomorphized in the form of Elena who "encompassed the city" (62), is also depicted as being tantalizingly "beautiful" but ultimately made up of lethal "illusions" (62) which hide the evil that is slowly consuming its soul. The contradiction is supplemented by a luminous, exotic, and vibrant city and through a description of social unrest, decay and stasis, which foreshadow impeding doom. Such provisionality rehearses the decentred subjectivities of Marco and the other characters: "Venice doubled and the three of them caught in the fulcrum of the doubleness" (138). Multi-faceted and highly fluid, the ancient city tenaciously resists closure: "Each stone in the city containing story over story, layer over layer of human history. Who could choose the essential one? The true one?" (170-171).

5. Gender Identities

The leitmotif of performance is used in the representation of gender as a component of ethnicity. Gender is constructed by an aggregation of interconnected, antagonistic, and ever-changing social determinants. In Canada, "femininity" is defined from a clustering of opposed, disjunctive, and unstable cultural models. Mrs. Bolcato insists that her daughter Bianca should accede to patriarchal womanhood and renounce her foolhardy independence. Helen Barolini claims that "[Italian immigrant] daughters assert a need for self-identity and want to free themselves from past patterns [but] in denying the value of the mother's role by their rebellion against it, they lay upon themselves a heavy and terrible conflict."[6]

The motif of the mask and the illusoriness of cultural identities resurface in the depiction of both traditional Italian and conventional Canadian femininity. Believing that her mother's "whole system of customs and beliefs was fake, a private fantasy, like the fairy tales" (84), Bianca assumes that the host society offers a more authentic and relevant form of femininity. The English Canadian female role model she turns to proves to be contradictory and misleading. Jody's mother is an ostensibly genteel and open-minded woman, who functions as a wife and mother. She is economically and socially dependent on her husband, and differs little from Bianca's mother, an unsophisticated working woman. North American popular culture actively promotes the values of conventional womanhood: "Loretta and I would . . . play out our latest fantasies with my Natalie Wood (her) and Sandra Dee (me) paper dolls" (80). Integration is hampered because the protagonist cannot accept the ideas and attitudes of a patriarchally-based English Canadian society. Catholic school represses the protagonist's sexuality by associating desire with deviant and violent behaviour. The meaning derived by Bianca and her friends from the gory tale of St. Maria Goretti (who chooses death instead of the loss of her virginity) ironically confirms the power of female sexuality: "A martyr to foul male lust . . . Her very presence had inflamed a man to violence" (109-110). This implied reinterpretation of the story temporarily preempts Catholicism's disapproval of female desire: "Sex was a basic appetite like hunger and thirst, and the satisfying necessary . . . The church had mounted an enormous scaffold of lies to control and oppress" (110).

Popular femininity is shown to reside in an elitist, hierarchical social system. Distancing herself from Bianca in order to consolidate her status among the daughters of affluent families, Jody upholds the group's decision to reject a fellow student's membership because of her ethnicity and social class. The subsequent relationship with Jack, who is of Ukrainian background, opens Bianca up sexually and frees her from Italian womanhood, but it also limits her to a socially-sanctioned femininity. The coincidence of Jack's traditional ethnic values with the gender suppositions of the mainstream infers that patriarchy moves across cultural boundaries. By disclosing the sham of romantic love, Bianca flags her resistance to the norms of the dominant culture: "the man and woman meet, they make love, they move in together, they discover indeed they are in love . . . he must be the much-awaited prince, she the lovely princess. There must be a happily-ever-after, a validation" (49).

The pull of ethnicity supplants the appropriation of a new feminine self. Wanting to rekindle her bond with a sickly Marco, Bianca imaginatively assumes the role of the nurturer: "Hold your hand, iron your shirt, tempt you back to food with homemade pasta . . . I could soothe" (52). Bianca's present life in Edmonton is played out against a backdrop of towering mountains and endless prairie. The allusions to a regenerative nature (linked to Bianca's creativity as a woman) hint at a curative feminine space.

This invocation of femaleness is part of Bianca's storymaking, and, as such, highlights the conscious reframing of identity and not the privileging of an essential femininity. Positioned within two mobile and incompatible cultural systems, the protagonist cannot unite her multiple feminine identities.

Gender as a series of social guises likewise pervades the Venetian narrative. The characters frequently emulate media-generated masculinity and femininity. Piero, Elena's comrade and lover in the revolutionary underground, consciously imitates the stylized aggressivity of fictional detectives on American television. Marco's stilted perceptions of the women in his life reproduce the sexual dichotomies of patriarchal culture. The virginal Paola, "a magazine cover bride[,] [s]o perfect in her elegant lace and silk, in the pearl coronet and the cascading floor length veil" (30), is contrasted to a coquettish Elena dripping with lust: "She slowly slid off her white fur jacket, pursing her red, red lips into a girlie magazine pout" (58). These stereotypical images of women indicate Marco's complicity with patriarchy. As Elena performs her role as a temptress, objectifying her body, Marco indulges in "crude [sexual] fantasies" (62).

The fabrication of gender identities is attached to a system of structured behaviour. Even after Elena sheds her disguise in the process of making love, Marco notes that "her reactions remained skilled, almost professional" (62). The emptiness of their lovemaking exposes the sterility of socially conditioned gender roles. Romantic love was "[the] surface titillation by programmed caresses, mental fantasies, or the vaporous sentiments of young lovers . . . [it was] the reflection of themselves in their lover's eyes that they loved . . . [it was] the postures, the trappings, the masks, they wanted" (100-101). Elena persists against sexual objectification and affirms the complexities of feminine identity: "behind her assigned role [she] became more fluid, more uncontainable" (62). Paola refuses to be a domestic and sexual servant. The falsity of Marco's furtive liaison with Elena splits open the distorting categories of patriarchy and reveals the arbitrariness and contigencies of masculinity.

Gender is contexualized within the parameters of Western society. While citing the male-centrism of the old world, Bianca implies that a woman is similarly constrained by the patriarchal strictures of Canadian society: " 'One difference between here and there is the men. In Canada, among educated people particularly,' I was exaggerating, lying almost, 'antiquated roles are passing away' " (150). Gender relations are portrayed as complex and contradictory. The female characters try to overcome their subordination by using their domestic functions to attain some leverage in their relationships or try to repudiate traditional notions of womanhood.

Domesticity and motherhood are key components to the maintenance of family, and contest the male's primacy, as illustrated by Tarquinio's deference to his wife in establishing the priorities of the household and Marco's sense of inadequacy in coping with his son's debilitating illness. Elena has opted out of conventional womanhood by divorcing her husband and by becoming involved in political subversion. In response to her lovers, Piero and Marco, Elena strategically assumes subservient feminine poses in order to undermine male control. Piero's macho posturing depends on the enactment of her female-based erotic/violent persona and Marco is deluded in his belief that he can master her sexually.

Bianca's representation of the male subject is similarly conflictive. Marco Bolcato operates in several categories simultaneously: his physicality and virility awaken young Bianca's adolescent desire, his sensitivity and emotionality give him an androgynous quality which transcends gender difference; his egoism, paternalism, and sexual infidelity confirm his patriarchal nature. Jack is likewise contradictorily depicted. He has an intuitive connection to the land and his natural physical presence allows Bianca to effortlessly express her sexuality. Yet he is a hyper-rationalist and adheres to conventional masculine values. Bianca's break up with Jack and her inability to communicate with her traditionally-minded cousin demonstrate her refutation of patriarchal masculinity: "Through her writing [Bianca Bolcato] finds that . . . her identity cannot be bound up with that of a man. Individual freedom and independence, especially as she finds them in Western Canada, are important for Bianca's development as a person."[7]

Bianca's narrative deconstructs established images of femaleness and affirms her autonomy as a woman. Yet the male subject, ambiguously embodied by Marco, is integral to her self-conscious exploration of ethnicity. The women in this novel unwittingly facilitate and vigorously subvert a patriarchally based maleness, blurring the line between victim and skilful opponent.

7

Fairy Tales and *Bottled Roses*

Deconstructing the Stereotypes

Darlene Madott's collection of short stories, *Bottled Roses*, involves episodes in the lives of a number of third generation Italian Canadian female protagonists who question and rethink their cultural/gender identities. While maintaining varying perspectives on immigration, immigrant culture, and femininity, these stories present a recurrent plot-line and the central characters often function as the narrators of their own stories. This thematic and formal similarity evokes a particular feminine consciousness, which encompasses differing viewpoints, and leads to a recurrent character type. This is the woman who has left her Italian Canadian boyfriend or husband and wants to extricate herself from what she considers to be the harmful influence of a residual patriarchal-matrifocal immigrant heritage. As she engages in the struggle, she attempts to forge a new way of life in English Canadian society and outside the parameters of conventional Italian womanhood. In contesting the values and world view of the old culture, she ironically confirms its signifying power in the constitution of identity. Both the protagonist's sceptical attitude towards immigrant history and tradition, and her tenuous positioning in the mainstream mirror the discontinuities and duplicities of ethnicity.

This view is also obvious in *Made in Italy* and *The Lion's Mouth* which in their own fashion depict the dilemmas of living within two male-centred cultures. *Bottled Roses* marks such perplexity and ambivalence by continually shifting from first to third person voice as it moves from story to story, alternately expressing the protagonist's closeness to and distance from herself and her Italian and Canadian social environments. The juxtaposition of divergent pictures of the Italian immigrant, the use of irony in the plot structure, and the image patterns of the stories underline the perspectival ambiguities of the protagonist.

The deconstructing of gender roles, the leitmotif of performance, and the interrogative posture of the main character point to the social construction of ethnicity and femininity. Both ethnicity and femininity are represented in non-essentialist terms, multi-layered, provisional, and contradictory. The stories are mostly anchored in the past; memory hints at the precariousness of cultural origins. These techniques together locate differences outside the self, in the areas between identities, and more importantly, within the multiple subjectivity of the female protagonist.

1. Juxtaposition, Irony, and Ethnicity

Contradictory portraits of the first generation Italian Canadian (the grandmother figure who incarnates the values and beliefs of the immigrant culture) transmit the incoherence of the ethnic subject. In the short story, "Bottled Roses," the grandmother's stories of depravation and stoic perseverance are meant to typify the immigrant experience. They are subverted by the protagonist's alternative reconstruction of the aged matriarch's life. Frugality during the difficult times of the Depression (in which grandmother Nicolina "made over old clothes") is offset by a description of well-fed guests who "ate meat while her own family filled up with bread."[1] The contrast insinuates that keeping up appearances, essential to the grandmother's sense of family honour, exacerbated the family's difficulties. Nicolina's claim that she has led a restrictive and gruelling life as a woman and as an immigrant is contested by the implication that she ran the household in a dictatorial fashion, hen-pecking her docile husband and sedulously controlling the behaviour of her children. Although Nicolina was forced to marry the man whom her father chose, ironically, she was opposed to the marriages of all her children. Nicolina is portrayed in anti-heroic terms as narrow-minded, devious, and self-centred. She is associated with stasis and decay, symbolic of the decline of the first generation's way of life: "everything about her was old and powerless — the room smelling of dust and bad breath and potted plants and those God-awful snake plants . . . her greyed doilies, the matted wig she hatboxed every night, her chipped teacups and her warped old ideas" (25-26). By contradicting Nicolina's stories, the protagonist consciously places herself against Italian culture.

The unfavourable portrait is undermined by Jean's admiration of her grandmother: "[She] was a formidable, Depression-made terror of a woman . . . [but] Nicolina Leone was more interesting than the whole pack of aunts and uncles put together" (6). She discerns in the elderly woman an aspect of her own personality, which is predisposed to grandiose gestures and emotional excess: "My grandmother and I shared an instinct for the theatre. That was what we saw in each other and it made a bond between us" (6). The decrepit grandmother becomes an indomitable and energetic individual who, at the age of ninety-three, is "still stubbornly entrenched in her own home" and "still turning the earth of the garden" (6). Reinforcing the narrator's bond with the old woman is her sympathetic acknowledgment of the widowed Nicolina's loneliness and isolation. Jean sadly realizes that her grandmother has been diminished physically and psychologically by old age. Equally significant is Jean's affirmation of feminine continuity, despite the differing viewpoints among the successive generations of women in the family: "I sense there is a pattern . . . that the four of us complete — my grandmother, my mother, myself and [my niece]" (6).

In "The Namesake," the protagonist-narrator simultaneously reconstructs and disputes, through a series of conflicting images, the truthfulness of Granny Giuseppina's story of her niece. Pina's alleged selfishness and ill-will towards others is undercut by an overbearing and ogre-like aunt, who harangues her niece about her dishevelled appearance and poor working habits. She views the niece as a freak of nature. The younger woman's disturbing reflection in the hand mirror is an ironic representation of Giussepina's own perception of herself: "Who had [Pina] seen when she had looked into my grandmother's mirror? Giusseppina's Pina or her own" (80).

The grandmother's reference to Pina as a dark, sinister creature and as a "black harbinger of death" (69) links her niece to numerous deaths in the family circle, and ironically evokes the stillbirth of her own child. As the twinning of their stories indicates, both women are caught in the same chain of domestic toil and are culturally isolated in the new world. Giussepina vents her anger and depression by pitilessly lashing out at her namesake for her neurotic behaviour. This displacement of emotion indicates the older woman's precarious positioning in her immigrant household, and points to the internal conflicts of ethnicity. It suggests that the pressures of adaptation in an arduous socioeconomic environment often result in familial strife. In crafting an ambivalent picture of the grandmother as victim and victimizer, the protagonist-narrator exposes the disjunctions of Italian Canadianness. Like "[Granny Giuseppina who] tells a great deal of [stories], shaded with the dark and light of her own morbid fascinations" (80), she also gives voice to the undecidedness of ethnic identity.

The adverse old world is also present in "Family Sacraments." Here Pasquale DiMarko, a staunch promoter of family and tradition, is described both as an authoritarian patriarch and as a warm, loving person. He corrects his wife's domestic activities, interferes in his daughter's marriage, and is estranged from his oldest son, who has been disowned as a member of the family. Franny, the protagonist, is Pasquale's house guest. She is subjected to his paternalism. Pasquale intrudes into her affairs. He is not scared to listen in on Franny's conversations on the phone with her family. In contrast to his wife, Maria, who bestowed her kindness "on everyone regardless of their natures" (35), Pasquale is viewed as an irascible, sometimes vengeful, and sanctimonious individual. This negative rendering of the Italian patriarch is juxtaposed to images of Pasquale as an affectionate, tender man. Pasquale's son-in-law is loyal to his dead wife, Lenora, and this is a testament to the strength of familial relations. Supplementing this depiction is Pasquale's lack of pretension, his pride in his home, and his self-sufficiency, which is displayed in his skill as a handyman and gardener.

The ambiguous depiction of the octogenarian reflects Franny's problematic cultural positioning. Her attempts to be a writer evince the same kind of commitment that allowed Pasquale to succeed in the new world. Both Franny and Pasquale are linked to the struggle, perseverance, achievement, and persistence of an entire community: "[His] kitchen table was to him what my desk was to me. It was where he ate and drank and saw what came of his labour . . . it was the scene of family and friendship, the daily intercourse of disappointment and joy" (36). Identification with family is imparted in the idealized tableau of the kitchen table. This identification appears to be the entry point into historical and cultural consciousness: "Home was what flowed in my veins, the essence of my people shored up for me in their hearts" (51). Subverting the privileging of family are images of entrapment in the DiMarko household. Franny is detached from Pasquale and Maria whose habits and values are often incompatible with those of mainstream society.

Franny's contradictory positioning is further expressed through ironic imagery. The basement apartment in the DiMarko home both imprisons her and acts as a comfortable retreat from the outside world, releasing her energies as a writer. This ambiguity is reiterated in the allusion to the blood-like colour of wine. Intense familial bonding and the separating of liquid from sediment indicate the diminution of Italianness in the new world. Juxtaposition and irony highlight the tenuous interlocking of cultural polarities: "There was something exasperating and joyous, oppressive and comforting, something in all of this I either wanted to understand, or to run away from" (36).

2. *Deconstructing Gender Identities*

The multi-positionality of the protagonist is recapitulated through the deconstructing and revising of Italian and Canadian gender identities. Again, the use of irony sets a up a complex signifying field which highlights the indeterminacy of the gendered subject. Linda Hutcheon submits that in women's writing "irony [is] a useful mode by which to acknowledge the force of [patriarchal] culture and yet to contest it, in perhaps covert but not ineffective ways."[2]

The representation of ethnicity and femininity betrays a constant tension between a dominating Italian female identity and that which exists outside of it. The central character's view of the world is influenced by mainstream gender models, which remain, nonetheless, unformed and indecisive. The ethnic maternal figure, whether the grandmother or immigrant mother, is frequently situated in the domestic sphere. She imperiously manages the household and controls the behaviour of her children. The representation of Italian femininity is contextualized within a specific social and historical framework.

Helen Barolini states that the immigrant woman's identity is bound to her functions in the household: "The Italian woman comes from a ... world in which her life was always dependent upon a male — her father, brother, husband, and, eventually, if widowed, her sons. Family was the focal point of her duty and concern, and, by the same token, the source of self-esteem and power, the means by which she measured her worth and was in turn measured, the reason for her being."[3]

It is precisely this form of dependent femininity against which the protagonist is reacting. This is what actively impedes a woman's independence and professional advancement. In "Bottled Roses," Paul's mother opposes Paul's marriage to Jean because the marriage will diminish her influence over him and devalue the legitimacy of her traditional role. Speculating about her future life with Paul, Jean reveals her own anxiety at the prospect of becoming an unimaginative and subservient woman.

Against an old world feminine identity, Madott places a definition of womanhood which contests the ideological premises of Italian patriarchy.

For Pia Pichini, second or third generation Italian Canadian women "have come to expect more sex role equality ... [and] want to break with traditional female stereotypes. They want the freedom to choose a career, marry and have children at their convenience, rather than to conform to the familial customs expected of them."[4] Madott's text challenges established stereotypical images of Italian femininity which valorize a history of physical-sexual depravation and social marginalization: "There is the silent suffering immigrant woman; the ignorant immigrant woman; the immigrant woman who accepts her submissive role . . . and the immigrant woman who stands as a symbol for Mother Italia, family, an entire culture."[5] By deconstructing stereotypes, Madott insists that "the oppression of women is often perpetuated by . . . first generation immigrant women [who] continued to enforce upon their daughters [and granddaughters] the same rules and roles given to them by their mothers."[6]

The critique of Italian femininity quickly veers off into caricature and, thereby, ironically reinstitutes the gender stereotype which Jean is subverting: "I'd picture myself twenty years from then buying purple sweaters and Woolco purses, the same dark fringe above my lips, standing in a field of dandelions with hands pressed against my back to keep my stomach from toppling me" (14). This derisive delineation of the immigrant woman is directly contradicted by the admission that, as a widowed parent and an immigrant woman, Paul's mother has had to cope with severe socioeconomic conditions: "she was alone, more alone than ever my grandmother had been when she undertook the same journey a half-century before" (13). Traditional womanhood which deploys its skills inside and outside the home to sustain the family unit is a strategy for survival and not just a self-serving perpetuation of a patriarchal-matrifocal order.

Through various representations of the immigrant woman, Madott suggests that gender relations swing back and forth between interdependency and irresolvable conflict. Ironically, Italian femininity cannot be so easily dispensed with because it constitutes an important part of the protagonist's gendered subjectivity: "I was terrified of ever coming to resemble that, and yet I was filled with what I hated" (14). The protagonist's Canadian identity does not supplant but continuously curves back and rejoins her Italian side.

The diverse representations of Italian masculinity as a serious obstacle to feminine autonomy as well as being a source of erotic desire accentuate the instability of the gendered subject. In the title story, Jean resists her Italian boyfriend's attempt to block her acting career and isolate her in the role of wife and mother. At the same time, she is drawn to him sexually and touched by his vulnerability. Jean's double gesture, in which she finds Paul complicit with old world patriarchy and cites his traumatic boyhood in Italy and Canada, reinforces her contradictory responses to Italian masculinity.

This ambivalence issues from an inconsistent, fluid cultural positioning. As a third generation Italian Canadian, Jean has not been subjected to the difficulties of immigration. She approaches ethnicity from within and without a Canadianized perspective. Although Paul reinforces Jean's Italian feminine self, he remains culturally and personally indefinable: "Half of his thoughts were in another language, forever foreign to me. Even the landscapes of his dreams . . . were . . . alien to me, who could never know the sound of a cypress from that of a pine" (13).

Cultural disjunction results in another ironic reversal. Jean is repelled by Paul's Canadianness, typied by his faith in science and technology and by his professional ambition as an engineer. But she is completely overtaken by his aggressive masculine presence, which she attributes to his Italian background: "as long as I could still see his face, burnt like a negative upon my mental plate, I had no will not to fly into that flame" (22). Jean participates in an endless process of combining, negating, and reworking numerous and always competing cultural/gender elements.

The valorizing of the sensuality and feelings of English Canadian males discloses the central character's wish to forge an alternative feminine self. Her interactions with admiring and supportive Canadian men permit the coming into consciousness of a gender identity that is organized around feminine desire and experience.

In "Waiting," lovemaking and couplehood bring Franny into contact with her own sexuality and foster a state of emotional reciprocity. When Franny was a young girl on the verge of adolescence, John Brown had an infatuation and devotion that made her aware of the potential power of her burgeoning femininity. This romantic tableau is quickly problematized by the impermanence and conflictedness of gender relations. On the rebound from a disastrous marriage to an Italian Canadian, Franny wants to fulfil her immediate sexual and emotional needs, but is neither willing nor prepared to make a commitment.

Waiting, the pervasive theme in the story, communicates the indeterminateness of the ethnically gendered subject. This waiting signals the instant before the transforming of feminine identity, and anticipates the possibility of a new and secure couplehood. It also emphasizes stasis and an inability to move past conditions that have stalled the consolidation of an alternative feminine self. Correspondingly, waiting signifies the conscious exclusion of Canadian masculinity, as embodied by the West Coast lover, in the reconceptualizing of ethnicity and femininity: "He looked like a man condemned and waiting the sentence" (92). This exclusionary gesture is repeated in "When John Brown And I Were Young" in which Franny's adolescent self is unappreciative of her admirer's friendship, and asserts her femininity by tactlessly dismissing his earnest demonstration of love.

The Canadian male is rendered as the cultural/gender other. In "Waiting," the male lover, who is unnamed and only referred to in the third person, belongs to "a separate and impenetrable world" (88) which avoids comprehensibility. The alterity of the Canadian male recurs in the last story of the collection, where Franny pointedly conveys her detachment from the boy next door: "John Brown was something apart from me, not a part of me, like an arm or leg" (106). The lack of closure in the two narratives further problematizes the relevance of Canadian masculinity to an ongoing, yet-to-be-determined feminine identity. In the concluding moment of "Waiting," the reunion of the lovers remains conjectural, suggesting still tentative cross-cultural gender relations. Reconsidering her rejection of John Brown, the protagonist is filled with regret and a sense of loss: "John Brown had offered me something whole and beautiful . . . I passed the place where he was waiting" (112). The intertextual meaning of waiting, as possibility and erasure, asserts the irresolution of the previous story. Madott implies ironically that Franny is moving away from a man who is supportive of her independence.

The disjunctive representation of Italian Canadian femininity includes an ironic reversal of gender/cultural positions. The Canadian male's sensitivity and lack of aggression allow a maneuverability denied to the protagonist in the relationship with her Italian Canadian partner. By asserting her sexual power in her affair with a Canadian male, Franny reenacts the dominating posture of her Italian Canadian lover. Still influenced by a traditionally-oriented Italian femininity, she unconsciously reactivates the psychological patterns inhering in old world patriarchy. The Vancouver encounter exposes the lingering puritanism of the ancestral culture, in which fidelity is considered to be axiomatic: "She thought it strange . . . that a man could love a woman who bore the signs of another upon her skin" (10).

Against this contradictory picture of the gendered subject, Madott gives us glimpses of an idealized heterosexuality. In "Family Sacraments," Greg encompasses the positive qualities of both old and new world masculinity. This is illustrated by his faithfulness to his dead wife, allegiance to family, natural physicality, and emotional sensitivity. Franny's parents' daily affirmation of their love and respect for each other repeats the merging of cultural elements. These redeeming gender relations mirror the easy sharing of affection between Pasquale and Maria DiMarko, and ironically reinstall the centrality of Italianness. There is, however, an inadequacy at the core of Italian Canadian heterosexuality manifested in Greg's self-limiting decision not to remarry, in Franny's mother's contestation of her own mother's authority, and in Pasquale's disquietingly paternalistic attitude towards his wife. The conflicted gender positionings within the ethnic community approximate the tensions in Franny's past relationship with an Italian Canadian male.

In "Bottled Roses," the instability of ethnic/gender identities topples the binarism of Italian and Canadian masculinities. This is characterized by the ostensible opposition of physicality/aggressivity to sensitivity/sensuality. Jean is implicated in two multi-layered and inconstant cultural topographies. The privileging of careerism in the creative arts links her, ironically, to her male Italian counterpart, whose professional accomplishments buttress his self-esteem and facilitate social mobility. Assimilation into the mainstream leads to an analytical view, illustrated in the protagonist's conscious and often detailed dissection of the behaviour of others. This rationalism is identified with Paul's fascination with the theoretical models of modern airspace technology, alluded to in "Bottled Roses." The description of the Italian male's physicality overlaps with images in "Waiting" of the West Coast lover who relishes sexual activity and frolics in nature. The putative cultural binaries break down as Jean and Franny rebuff, absorb, abandon, and recompose various parts of Italian Canadian femininity. Identity formation signifies the disassembling of ethnicity since each cultural/gender framework is relative, contradictory, heterogeneous, and infinitely changeable.

3. Role-playing

The figuring of gender as social construction calls attention to the ways that ethnicity and femininity are constituted in relation to specific cultural practices. Traditional Italian femininity is effected through the performance of a historically scripted role: "I had a vision of the women in our family all giving birth to the same story, a tale that each successive generation must play out without anything ever being learned or redeemed" (25).

Interpenetrated by numerous social conditions, role-playing tends to be unpredictable and incongruous. In "Bottled Roses," the grandmother takes on the expected part as the family matriarch with theatrical aplomb, but is often at variance with this role. She is also depicted as a tired and spiritually defeated widow. In comparison, the granddaughter assumes a variety of temporary guises: the dutiful family member, compliant lover, and independent woman. Jean is always conscious that others around her are acting out several speaking parts.

This also is illustrated in "Waiting" by the designation of Franny's Canadian partner as a companion, lover, and father. Gender identities seem tentative and illusory. They are disconnected from the inner states of the performing subject. The story "Waiting" hints at the tentativeness of Franny's familial moment with her lover and young son: "To look at them, you might almost think they were a family coming home from the beach, sunburnt and spent" (97).

Role-playing is associated with images from popular culture. It is also deceptive since it conceals the antagonism of gender relations. In "John Brown," Franny characterizes her friend's mother as "a strange and beautiful lady we all thought was a Movie Star" (107). She imagines her absent husband is an adventurer, "a man in a Hudson's Bay jacket with a soft beard, incredibly handsome and gentle" (107). These romanticized images are overturned by subtle allusions to marital estrangement and parental neglect.

Similarly, in "Instructing the Young," the story of Cinderella and her Prince Charming, in which the fabled characters function as gender role-models, presents a deceptive picture of femininity and masculinity. Images of a marginalized Italian woman, worn-out by domestic labour, repeated pregnancies, and child-rearing, and of her overbearing, coarse husband are juxtaposed to the scene of the central character reading the fairy tale to the couple's obstreperous son. The jarring contrast is defused as the story shows the thematic linkage between the two frames of reference. The fairy tale's subjoining of femininity to masculinity concurs with Eva's subordinate position in her marriage to Luciano. Identification with prevailing images of gender is displayed by young Davide's mimicry of his uncle's flirtatious behaviour towards Julie and his imaginative entry into the Cinderella story. This is intrinsic to the cultural production of masculinity and femininity. The fairy tale is contradictory, for it suggests the protagonist's complicity with, and eventual repudiation of, the dominating patriarchal order.

Role-playing, however, necessitates a continuous acquisition and reinvention of cultural/feminine identities. This provisionality is transmitted through the recurring motifs of stage-acting and storytelling. In "Bottled Roses," Jean's career as an actress emblematizes the multiplicity of social roles: "I've rounded my life out in many roles, and I've enjoyed playing many people" (27). Each assumed role is but one aspect of her identity and therefore ultimately partial and uncertain: "But what do you really know of my life ? . . . What right do you think you have to play upon this one story? . . . You haven't heard the whole of me?" (27-28)

Fictiveness also highlights the reassembling of self-images and the appropriating of different and conflicting perspectives. In "The Namesake," the fluctuation in cultural positioning is evidenced through the narrator's contrary depiction of her grandmother as victim and victimizer. Her diverse responses to her grandmother's story range from incredulity to outright revulsion. In "Family Sacraments," Franny's interpretation of the love story between Greg and Lenora oscillates between admiration and incredulity. She, in fact, communicates her proximity to and distance from Italian culture. Storytelling entails the constant deconstructing and reinscribing of personal identity.

4. *Open-ended Narration*

The inquisitive stance of the central character enunciates the incertitude attached to the notions of ethnicity and femininity. Each story addresses a particular event in her life by launching an inquiry into its underlying significance. Past experiences are held up for inspection in the hope that they will indicate the development of a coherent identity. The use of the interrogative initiates a movement back into the past. Questions are constantly repeated which have been posed to Jean in "Bottled Roses" — "Do I remember him?" (5) — or Franny queries the reason behind her actions in "Family Sacraments": "Why I undertook that journey west the summer I was twenty-six is something I haven't entirely understood yet" (29). Interrogation is an implicit component of the discourse on gender roles in "Instructing the Young" and of the conflict between opposed ideas of femininity in "The Namesake."

The reconstruction of past events brings under scrutiny the suppositions of mainstream culture. This is exhibited in the reexamination of the meaning of Franny's relationships with English Canadian males in "Waiting" and "John Brown." Questioning does not yield clear answers but incites more questions, opens more gaps, and reinforces the disunity and open-endedness of Italian Canadian identity. "[W]hat it does to me to remember?" Jean states in "Bottled Roses," "[Do] I now believe it harder to live with one loud, unretractable word than with all the walking shadows of might-have-beens?" (28)

Remembrance sporadically alternates between the use of the past and present tense. It indicates the immediacy of past events, but also underlines the irresolution of the gendered subject. In "Bottled Roses," Jean moves to the present tense when she recollects her decision to cancel her wedding: "The only two realities converge in my brain. Must call him. Must go" (22). This technique is redeployed in "Instructing the Young." At the very moment when reading the Cinderella story to her boyfriend's nephew, Julie realizes that her impending marriage to her Italian Canadian fiancee is a trap. The use of the present tense dramatically stresses disjunction. (Julie must break away from a patriarchally-based femininity.) It also, paradoxically, reinserts Italianness as an important element in the meaning of the text. Madott suggests that ethnicity is still a constituent part of Julie's identity. Retrospection sets up a picture of a woman in transition, who is unsteadily positioned between the traditional way of life and the surrounding mainstream culture with its promise of individual freedom.

8

Conclusion

Form, Identity, and Present and Future Trajectories

The various literary texts examined in this study indicate that Italian Canadian identity is multifaceted, contradictory, and indeterminate. The ethnic subject confronts incompatible values and attitudes which emanate from various parts of the immigrant-based community and the surrounding mainstream society. In the case of the female subject, cultural conflict is interwoven with issues about gender relations. Ideas about femininity and masculinity are located in specific and opposed cultural contexts. This antagonism is countered by the commingling and overlayering of diverse cultural and gender perspectives.

Affected by given social contexts, ethnicity involves several subject positions which simultaneously contest and interact with each other. While these subject positions can be complementary, they also maintain their quality of difference. The protagonist moves among a range of contending and adjoining viewpoints and is reluctant to embrace entirely any one of them. Such a lack of commitment leads to a form of detachment. Yet the protagonist continues to identify with aspects of the two cultural milieux because they reinforce his/her perceptions of reality. These underlying connections encourage a reinvestment in the ways of life of the two communities. Reentry, however, reactivates a series of ongoing contradictions and discontinuities. As the discussed literary texts demonstrate, resistance and attraction frequently characterize the protagonist's ambivalence towards both the minority group and mainstream society. In having to choose from a spectrum of available options, the protagonist is reminded of the relativity and limitations of any social and gender position.

The identity of the Italian Canadian subject is perpetually shaped and altered by variables which move across many cultural terrains. This lack of fixity suggests that identity is unclosed and engaged in persistent change. Homi Bhabha notes in his discussion of ethnicity that "the signs of cultural difference cannot then be unitary or individual forms of identity because their continual implication in other symbolic systems leaves them 'incomplete' or open to cultural translation."[1] In Italian Canadian fiction, ethnic subjectivity is partially affected by a specific social environment. Homi Bhabha insists that "the transfer of meaning can never be total between differential [cultural] systems of meaning, or within them."[2] Such inconclusiveness is characteristic of ethnic subjectivity in Italian Canadian writing. Speaking of minority literature, Bhabha observes that "it is the articulation through incommensurability that structures all narratives of identification."[3]

Minority texts, like those written by Italian Canadians, tend to reject an essentialist reading of culture and experience. In the words of Sneja Gunew, this kind of "approach lifts us out of mutually stabilizing binary binds and offers no neutral spaces to anyone."[4] Italianness as a marker of ethnic affiliation is not represented as a static concept but as something that is endlessly making and unmaking itself in multiple social contexts. Eduardo Galeano believes that a "national culture is defined by its content, not by the origin of its elements. Alive it changes incessantly, it challenges itself, it contradicts itself, and it receives external influences that at times increase it, and that are wont to operate simultaneously as a threat and a stimulus."[5] Italianness in the new world is shaped by complex and ever-changing cultural forces.

1. *Representational Strategies and Themes*

Italian Canadian writing employs a variety of strategies to represent the multiple and contradictory subject positions of the protagonist. Through the ironic treatment of plot and characterization, this fiction exposes conflicting and inconsistent beliefs and views. The dilemma of developing a new identity is central to the ironic representation of ethnicity. As Linda Hutcheon notes, "the drive towards self-definition within a new culture may well involve separation from [the] ethnic past, at least temporarily. And irony is a useful device for articulating both the pull of that tradition and the need to contest it."[6] Irony is inclusive in its depiction of Italian Canadian experience, invoking the numerous cultural outlooks that comprise ethnic subjectivity. In highlighting contradiction, heterogeneity, and the shifting of subject positions, irony suggests that the identity of the protagonist is indeterminate.

Similarly, the ambiguities which are generated through the use of the elegiac mode signify a lack of resolution. Elegy mixes together nostalgia, loss, separation, and redemption. These contradictory positions indicate that the homeland is not seen as an ideal place or as being solely responsible for the plight of its inhabitants.

Underlying this uncertain view of the past is an awareness, as result of immigration, of the impermanence of cultural patterns. Such instability is reiterated through the use of juxtaposition. The opposition of divergent and culturally charged images suggest a clash of beliefs between the old and new social orders as well as a contesting of values within them. Juxtaposition also emphasizes the interconnectedness of numerous cultural viewpoints. Contrast sets up the perspectival ambiguities of the protagonist as he/she straddles two cultural systems.[7]

Italian Canadian writing utilizes an assortment of other strategies to dramatize its exploration of the complexities of identity formation. Narrative form is often manipulated to embody the plural states of the protagonist through such devices as the double narrative, the use of the Remembering I and the Remembered I, and the intersecting of separate story lines. This fiction also makes symbolic use of various images which evoke the qualities of the two adjoining cultures.

The production of imagery is complemented by the refashioning of cultural mythologies in order to convey an interpretation of the past and to make sense of present circumstances. Linked to this strategy is an investigation of the shortcomings of both immigrant culture and mainstream society. The avoidance of sentimentality and cultural idealism supports the rendering of the difficulties of immigration and the process of adjustment, and the references to challenging socioeconomic conditions in the old country.

The documenting of extratextual reality serves to contextualize Italian Canadian experience and maintain its historical and social distinctiveness. The reconstruction of lived experience is reinforced by the use of memory as a way to invoke the material forces which have moulded the identity of the protagonist. Role-playing further develops the idea that Italian Canadianness is composed of a series of diverse and culturally specific subject positions. These representational strategies advance the view that ethnic subjectivity is socially constructed and not the sum of natural attributes.

Using a combination of the preceding formal strategies, each work of fiction offers a particular treatment of the multiplication of the ethnic subject. In Frank Paci's *Black Madonna*, the dramatization of the conflict between parents and children and between brother and sister permits an examination of various and differing responses to the pressures of adjustment. The Barone family mirrors the tensions and incongruities of daily life in Little Italy in Sault Ste. Marie. The novel describes a shift in perspective among the adult children as they grapple with the process of Canadianization. Through the linked narratives of Joey and Marie Barone, *Black Madonna* presents ethnicity as the constant interplay of competing and contradictory forces. In constructing new identities, the two protagonists have to recontextualize their Italianness in an ever-changing cultural landscape.

Other Selves, by C.D. Minni, is concerned with depicting the psychological states of outsidership among immigrant and second generation characters. In the text, immigration remains the defining moment since the effects of cultural dislocation cut across the generations. Unable to recreate old cultural patterns in an extremely dissimilar social environment, the protagonists find themselves at the periphery of both cultural contexts. In Canada the immigrant characters long for the past, but when they return home they discover that they no longer have a strong connection to the place they left behind. This uncertainty is repeated in the portrayal of the second generation characters. The shortcomings of an urban-based lifestyle bring them back to the immigrant enclave that they had abandoned in their youth. Yet traditional family values do not provide a way out of their marginalization in mainstream society. The many selves of the protagonists intersect but ultimately avoid convergence.

Nino Ricci's *Lives of the Saints* suggests that peasant culture is itself disunified and contradictory, since it has been and continues to be influenced by numerous social and economic forces. The disparities and instability of village life in Valle del Sol imply that Italianness in the old world is discontinuous and mutable. Immigration provides the peasants a means to escape their harsh economic predicament, and entails another process of transformation. The story of Vittorio Innocente and his mother, Cristina, uncovers the antagonisms and complexities of a society that is being reshaped by an oncoming modernity. Italianness is represented as a multi-levelled construct and, thus, is not reducible to a specific set of traits and attitudes. Immigration to Canada is supposed to herald a better way of life for Vittorio and his mother, and is undermined by the tragic nature of the trans-Atlantic crossing. Cristina's death signifies both the lingering, destructive power of the old culture and the trauma of resettlement. The devastating event reinforces the text's unromantic view of the homeland and hints at the narrator-character's disillusionment with the host country.

Such ambivalence is reiterated by Maria Ardizzi through the narrative of an immigrant woman. Economic deprivation and patriarchal tyranny in rural and small-town Abruzzi precede social dislocation and familial breakdown in consumer-driven, suburban Toronto. In contrast, the experience of female camaraderie on the Moratti farm during the war merges with Nora's economic independence in industrial society. Ardizzi intimates that immigration and the process of adjustment result in several discordant cultural/gender positions. The sense of homelessness that pervades Nora's autobiography underscores the indeterminacy of the ethnic subject in the new world.

Told from the perspective of a Canadianized protagonist, Caterina Edwards' *The Lion's Mouth* explores how ideas about identity and femininity are transmitted within specific social contexts. Ethnic subjectivity is formed by a spectrum of opposed cultural factors which are unstable and discrepant. Role-playing in the novel serves as an expression of the constructedness of the protagonist's ethnic/gender identity. Each social environment to which Bianca Bolcato is exposed imposes limitations on her behaviour. Not only do Venice and Edmonton promote male-centred notions about femininity, they also are corrupted by political and economic elitism. At the same time, both societies facilitate Bianca's resourcefulness and inspire her as a writer. Italian Canadianness as embodied by the protagonist appears to be multifaceted and inconsistent.

The impact of competing models of femininity on the lives of third generation Italian Canadian female characters is a crucial part of the representation of ethnicity in Darlene Madott's *Bottled Roses*. Distanced from their immigrant heritage because of their assimilation into mainstream society, and because of their rejection of traditional Italian womanhood, the protagonists attempt to develop a new sense of self according to contemporary English Canadian values. However, transformation does not eradicate immigrant-based attitudes which constitute a critical component of the protagonists' ethnic/gender identities. Although they are aware that their roles as women have been socially scripted, the characters cannot resist the powerful and conflicting influences of the encompassing cultural systems. Like the other cited texts, *Bottled Roses* insinuates that ethnicity is comprised of intricate subject positions which are unfixed and prevent closure.

2. *Ethnic Subjectivity and Literary Discourse*

The representation of the multiple and open-ended cultural position of the minority subject avoids an essentialist and limited reading of ethnic identity. The work of Frank Paci,

C.D. Minni, Nino Ricci, Maria Ardizzi, Caterina Edwards, and Darlene Madott does not invoke a universalized and timeless Italian Canadian identity. These texts confirm that there are no all-encompassing and unchanging attributes that constitute Italianness and Canadianness. Italian Canadian identity is composed of a series of variables which at different times and in different contexts oppose, complement, and modify each other. The emphasis on multiplicity and transformation counters a romanticizing and reification of ethnicity, and permits an understanding of the complex forces which shape the perspective of the ethnic subject.

Of equal importance is that, in the cited literary texts, the attitudes and behaviour of the ethnic characters are not reducible to a grouping of cultural stereotypes. Characters are intertwined in a contradictory and unpredictable social environment. The various Italian-descended protagonists hold a spectrum of beliefs which ironically connects them to, but also separates them from, other members in the Italian community and from the surrounding social order. Heterogeneity is reinforced by the fact that individuals enter Italian and Canadian culture in ways that differ markedly from the behaviour of other members of the ethnic community. Cultural retention and assimilation are experienced inconsistently, partially, and at numerous levels by the characters. The perceptions of what is of value in mainstream society are also varied and, at times, radically opposed to each other. Canadianness, therefore, for the fictional characters is an unfixed and highly interpretative concept.

These representations of ethnic subjectivity reject a universal view of ethnicity and refuse stereotypical ideas about Italian identity and mainstream society. They suggest that the protagonists are not influenced solely by their ties to the ancestral culture. In deconstructing and making relative the ethnic background of the protagonists, the writers imply that the identity of any cultural group, whether it is Italian Canadian or English Canadian, is equally multiple and unstable. The novels and short story collections, however, do not promote the view that historical-cultural factors which locate the ethnic subject in a specific ethnic community are secondary to the development of a social and personal identity. They do not insinuate that the experiences of the Italian-descended characters are interchangeable with the cultural experiences of others who are non-Italians.

In their work, the six writers do not eradicate the salient cultural markers which signify that the Italian Canadian protagonists are different from members of other ethnic communities. The surrounding English-based social order which is part of the daily lives of the characters is represented contradictorily as something that is simultaneously familiar and distant. It is the constant tension between the Italian-centred and English Canadian components of the minority protagonists' identities that continually reinstates the notion of ethnicity. Ethnic subjectivity never discards its connections to the original culture. Instead, it constantly reframes and rethinks its cultural heritage, not only to fit into a new socioeconomic setting, but also because the original culture is itself always involved in a process of reformulation.

In this sense, the Italian Canadian literary text resists being absorbed into a larger and all-embracing cultural discourse. While the text imaginatively reconstructs and reinterprets such sociological conditions as immigration, social adjustment, assimilation, intra-family conflict, and socioeconomic relations with the dominant social order, it includes in its discourse ideas, attitudes, and vantage points that have come out of these specific historical moments which generally still hold sway at some level in the Italian community. In maintaining its social and historical particularity, the Italian Canadian text declares its resistance to cultural homogenization and clears a space for the reinvention of Italianness in the new social order.

Although ethnic writing goes beyond a mere literary depiction of sociological processes, it insinuates that its content is not culturally and ideologically neutral. This lack of neutrality is manifested through its insistence on reconstructing an identifiable social milieu with its attendant assumptions and beliefs. The various meanings of the text are linked to a host of cultural signifiers which are specific to the experiences, albeit diverse and frequently contradictory, of the members of a particular ethnic community. Also the Italian Canadian literary text attempts to revise prevailing ideas about Canadianness, often through the contrasting and overlapping of opposed cultural perspectives.

This recontextualizing of Canadianness takes place within a localized ethnic experience, and implies that the ethnic text does not just critique and modify existing cultural notions, but actually creates new ways of perceiving and behaving. Canadianness in this context is no longer associated solely with an established and dominant English Canadian social group. It is a concept and a mode of being that comprises the social topography of the ethnic subject. Different forms of Canadianness are contemplated which are not necessarily connected to English Canadian based beliefs and attitudes. The representation of Canadianness suggests that ethnic literature is not a subset of a larger literary discourse on the nature of Canadian reality.

By announcing its cultural particularities, the Italian Canadian text, like other types of minority writing, asserts that ethnicity is a constituent feature of contemporary Canadian society. It also posits, by implication, that English Canadian literature, at some level of its representation, is culturally-specific and that even the omission of any reference to other cultural group experience is itself a confirmation of its cultural specificity.

The ethnic text, however, cannot easily dissociate itself from the dominant cultural context. In Italian Canadian fiction, often English Canadian characters are either of secondary importance or peripheral to the plot, if not entirely absent. Yet the fictional reconstruction of an Italian Canadian milieu is unable to bypass references to the dominant culture. The values and attitudes of the mainstream are almost always embedded in the consciousness of the ethnic protagonist.

The literary expression of a minority perspective does not depend just on the execution of certain formal strategies. While technique is not value-free and is loaded with ideas about the structuring of reality, in ethnic writing the differences between modes of realist and non-realist representation often do not reflect in general terms a radical divergence on the nature of ethnic identity.

Except for *The Lion's Mouth*, the other Italian Canadian texts examined in this study follow a conventional narrative line. The use of the traditional narrative does not imply a view of the world that is coherent, stable and aims at some form of closure. Literary representation in Italian Canadian writing tends to rely on a discourse about the multiplication of the subject which derives from a complex cultural context. As this analysis of Italian Canadian fiction has maintained, ethnic subjectivity is represented as provisional, multiple, and unfixed.

However, in ethnic writing literary form is not of secondary importance. It is a crucial part of the transmission of meaning. Certain formal patterns and narrative techniques have been used in such a way as to carry cultural signifiers and to develop the themes of the given text. As Antonino Mazza notes, an ethnic writer does not abandon literary tradition and influence in order to provide only a social document of a particular ethnic experience. Instead, he or she joins together various literary influences, some indigenous to specific regional localities in Italy and others belonging to a wider Western literary tradition, to construct a vision of the world.[8] Mazza contends further that an ethnic writer presents a poetic or imaginative view of reality and that the deploying of assorted literary devices is intrinsic to the advancement of this view.

The creation of a new mythology which combines traditional forms of living and creative expressions from the past with new modes of being and new methods of articulating imaginative experiences in the present is a central part of ethnic writing. The creative act is a means to fashion a new reality for the ethnic subject: "when we remember we re-invent our past, we invent what we need . . . The imagination orients us into the new habitat."[9]

The envisioning of identity and the inventing of new models of identity while they are related to specific extratextual factors are vital elements in the imaginative landscape of the ethnic text. Although the six texts attempt to investigate and deconstruct social reality, they are in themselves imaginative expressions of Italianness in Canada and not merely social documents of ethnic experience.

The challenge, then, to conducting a critical analysis of ethnic writing lies in the connecting of the cultural context to the imaginative realm. This has to be done without privileging content over form and without divesting the text of its cultural particularity which makes it distinct from other kinds of literary expressions. Italian Canadian writing both withstands cultural homogenization and cannot be characterized simply as a type of literary sociology.

3. Possible Future Directions

The critical study of Italian Canadian literature is still largely in its developmental stages. There are many areas of analysis which can possibly be undertaken. It would be useful to examine the various formal influences present in the literature, focusing on specific literary forms which are rooted in the indigenous culture, as well as other influences which have been appropriated through exposure to European/North American literary traditions and currents. This study could result in a better understanding of what constitutes an Italian Canadian literary aesthetic. It would provide an understanding of the effects of the cross-fertilization of formal techniques on the representation of Italianness in Canada.

Another possible area of analysis would be to compare Italian Canadian writers on the basis of their regional Italian backgrounds, such as Friuli, Abruzzi, Calabria, and Sicilia. This comparison could open up a discussion as to whether there is a regional Italian sensibility present in the work of the selected writers and what this would mean in the depiction of Italian Canadian experience. Another important endeavour would be to examine how orality is translated into literary language and to assess in formal and cultural terms the results of the interaction between the oral and the written. Equally worthwhile would be a comparison of the work of female and male Italian Canadian writers with the aim of exploring differences in formal patterns, chief among them is the use of imagery and differences in points of view, in order to discern a gendered representation of Italianness.

There could be a comparison of relatively older writers, such as Frank Paci, C. D. Minni, Antonio D'Alfonso, Marisa Di Franceschi, Caterina Edwards, and Mary Melfi, with younger ones; for example, Fiorella De Luca Calce, Carol David, and Nino Ricci. This comparison would allow the critic to see formal differences, as well as a divergence of perspectives. There could also be genre and cross-genre studies of Italian Canadian literature to provide a sense of the employment and development of form in fiction, poetry, and drama, and to discover whether the use of a particular genre entails a difference in perspective.

There is also a need to do an in-depth comparative study of different ethnic literatures in Canada in order to situate Italian Canadian writing in a broader discourse on ethnicity. Such a study could chart formal and thematic similarities and differences with the purpose of trying to arrive at an idea of what constitutes an ethnic literary aesthetic in Canadian literature.

These proposed investigations also would keep in mind the need to turn to various methodologies in order to expand the critical understanding of Italian Canadian literature. Culturally-based and discursive analyses of literary texts should be complemented with formal and theoretical approaches. This inclusiveness would allow a wider scope to the examination of the many ways that ethnic subjectivity is represented in Italian Canadian writing.

9

Theoretical Afterword

Minority Writing, Culture, Agency, and Representation

The critical study of Italian Canadian literature, especialy organized around the idea of cultural identity and its ideological and formal expressions, opens up important theoretical issues which are relevant to minority literature in general. Analysis of minority writing entails the use of different methodologies which include the many levels at which the literature operates; the literary, the cultural, the social, and the historical. This strategy underlines a crucial point: the acknowledgement of the multiple elements and operations of the minority text that makes it a distinct act of literary activity and separates it from the ideological intent, and even at times from the formal patterns of the dominant literature.

The difficulty in examining ethnic texts arises not only in deciding what should be the most important component of the analysis. It is a challenge to try to consider the various aspects of minority texts without bypassing the central concerns espoused in the work. Although the study of ethnic Canadian literature often has incorporated literary and sociological approaches, it has tended to focus on the diverse representations of identifiable sociological processes. Within the larger critical discourse in English Canada, the emphasis on literary sociology at times has put into question the literary and aesthetic merits and the thematic relevance of minority writing. This deprioritizing of the literary has been partly the result of the deeply politicized nature of canonization. It also has been the consequence of separating, theoretically speaking, the literary from the social plane or of attempting to privilege one over the other.

In current critical and cultural studies, the boundaries between disciplines have not only been disputed, but also they have been actively transgressed. New Historicism advances the study of literary texts with a multi-disciplined orientation, underscored by the idea that knowledge of history is crucial to the gleaning of the many meanings of literary texts. New Historicism "brackets together literature, ethnography, anthropology, art history, and other disciplines and sciences, hard and soft."[1] For the practitioner of New Historicism, "social and cultural events commingle messily" and there are "innumerable trade-offs . . . competing bids and exchanges of culture."[2] While literary texts offer up particular interpretations and reconstructions of histories and world views, they remain situated in specific social and cultural contexts. In his examination of literary texts as producers of cultural and social ideologies, Terry Eagleton insists that "history, one might say, is the ultimate specifier of literature, as it is the ultimate signified. For what else in the end could be the source and object of the signifying practice but the real social formation which provides its material matrix?"[3]

Texts, especially literary texts, are positioned within certain ideological and social parameters. As such, an analysis of the ways that these parameters are represented in texts is integral to the discernment of the meanings generated by texts. "For texts, as manifestations and expressions of social and gender relations, themselves constitute sets of relations," notes Elizabeth Fox-Genovese, "not relations innocent of history, but essentially historical relations of time, place, and domination. And without a vital sense of the structure of those relations, the reading of texts collapses into arcane, if learned and brilliant trivia."[4] Janet Wolff observes in her book, *The Social Production of Art,* that although "a sociology of art and culture seems to counterpose [the] two concepts [of 'structure' and 'creativity'], or at the very least to hold them in tension . . . they are not in fact in competition, but a proper understanding of each will expose their mutual interdependence."[5] Literary texts are located in and affected by particular social, cultural, and historical contexts. Cultural specificity is not just embedded in the discursive and formal structures of minority texts.

At some level of representation, all literary texts transmit culturally-specific meanings that connect them to particular histories and social formations. Minority texts evoke social and cultural environments that differ from those depicted in the work of English Canadian writers or of writers who have integrated into the dominant English-based social context. The importance of this cultural distinctiveness is lessened when ethnic texts are treated solely as a type of literary sociology. At times the cultural milieu of minority texts is of interest precisely because these texts are part of a larger investigation of sociological processes in English Canada. These texts do not necessarily become the focus of study because they have unique modes of reconstituting, through their representations of experience, significant facets of Canadian society and identity. Arnold Itwaru's statement on the work of several ethnic Canadian writers underscores the epistemological trajectory of minority texts: "Each of the novels selected [in my book] presents a number of versions of Canadian reality which in many ways go beyond the political, traditional, sociological and journalistic notions of Canada."[6] The compartmentalization of the inquiry into minority texts within the realm of "ethnic studies" (the term is being used here to demarcate a kind of critical orientation instead of a disciplinary-specific approach) tends to exclude literary concerns and minimizes the importance of minority texts as acts of representation in contemporary Canadian literary discourse. There is an emphasis on the social and cultural content of minority texts as a means of deciphering the signifying system of the texts. (The signifying system includes, for instance, imagery, symbolism, forms of narration, the use of irony and juxtaposition, and the reworking of mythic patterns.) This stress reinforces unwittingly the view that minority literature only uses poetic and fictional techniques as vehicles to describe various sociocultural phenomena.

Minority experience issues from a complex and conflictual socioeconomic landscape, stratified according to region, culture, race, social class, and gender. This situation makes obvious the lack of cultural and social homogeneity in Canada.

Arnold Itwaru insists that "it is the absence of a centralizing and unifying symbol which has necessitated differential inventions of meaning out of the experience loosely termed 'Canadian.'"[7] This is not to deny the existence of Canadian history and society. But it is essential to emphasize that there are differing and opposed views of what constitutes that history and social relations in Canada. The writing of Canadian history and the characterizing of social relations is a deeply politicized activity motivated by ideology and social class. Speaking about the current rewriting of Canadian history, Robin Mathews maintains that the "deconstruction of the myths that lead Canadians to accept U.S. metanarratives is absolutely necessary in order to redefine colonial history in this country."[8] Ethnic writing presents many interpretations of Canadianness and contests the varied and at times conflicting English-centred readings of social reality. What is often secondary or at the periphery of mainstream Canadian historiography is at the core of minority texts: considerations of culture and cultural differences. Minority texts are ideological expressions of Canadianness and not just narratives about the immigrant experience and the issue of cultural placement. The stress on the sociological in the study of ethnic texts shortcircuits the transmission of meaning and limits their intellectual reception. Minority writing tends to be looked at for its social content, the descriptions of and allusions to ethnic-specific conditions, and not necessarily for the subtleties and complexities of its representations.

Such an emphasis on the social also has the effect of suggesting that this literature develops themes and cites problems that are ancillary to the status quo, especially since cultural difference is often the concern of members of ethnic communities. Minority texts appear to be preoccupied with certain influences from the past, because ethnicity locates its references in specific historical social relations. The leitmotifs of minority narratives (tradition, immigration and the process of adjustment, intra-family and intra-group affiliation, interaction with the new society, and the rethinking of identity) indicate that the subjectivity of the ethnic protagonist is shaped by a host of historical and social forces and that the present is inextricably bound up by these forces. Minority texts often critique technology, urbanism, and consumerism, pointing to the excesses of corporate capitalism and the insularity and solipsism of individualism as evidence of the weakness of communal ties and the paucity of spiritual values. The criticism of the limitations and failures of the old world and the highlighting of the contradictory and unfixed nature of ethnicity in the new social order do not in themselves diminish the refutation of prominent aspects of contemporary English Canadian capitalist society. In minority texts, the representation of Canadianness brings together ideology and culture since the beliefs, values, and structures of the host country are contextualized within an English-based social order.

Mainstream fictional texts invoke multiple and contradictory versions of English Canadianness, critiquing, rejecting, and revising the nature of English Canadian culture. Canadian society is shaped by the conflicting politics of class, gender, race and ethnicity and by divisive regional and continental forces. English Canadians have become increasingly influenced by American society and their steady absorption both politically and culturally of American style individualism has shifted them away from their European heritage which put greater stress on collectivity. James Laxer contends that this Americanization has intensified with the free trade agreement and that "a comprehensive union with the United States . . . will require Canadians adopt American approaches not only to the economy but also to society and politics."[9] The socioeconomic cleavages in Canada indicate a diverse and conflicted national culture. Despite this strife and heterogeneity, mainstream English Canadian literature still operates within a dominating and larger historically and culturally specific framework. At some level, the literature confirms, in its referentiality and discourse, the value of English Canadianness. Often mainstream texts do not develop their settings, plots, themes, and characterizations to include the portrayal of a multicultural and multiracial society and to encompass the cultural-ideological positions that are part of this social reality.

Minority writing scrutinizes not just the features and merits of an English-centred culture. It also emphasizes the persistence of the old culture, despite the fact that it is often radically transformed by its association with the new social order. It is this ideological and cultural uniqueness that makes it difficult to integrate ethnic texts into mainstream literary discourse, because they continually call attention to their ethnicity, to their cultural difference, and thus to their expressed or implied resistance to the hegemonic proclivities of the dominant culture.

Aside from the issue of aesthetic value, which is attached to a culturally-specific criteria about what constitutes literary achievement, the breaking off of the literary from the cultural creates theoretical problems, because such a separation insinuates that the imaginative rendering of events does not participate in the same social process through which reality is constructed and through which particular experiences are invested with meaning. The treatment of minority texts from a sociological bent, while it maintains before us the cultural specificity of the texts, can be as limiting as a pure literary analysis of these texts, because a sociological analysis diminishes the significance of the representational strategies of minority texts. Representation cannot be reducible to social documentation in the same way that the sociological component of minority texts cannot be perceived simply as a subjective explanation of lived experiences.

Terry Eagleton's view that history enters a text as ideology,[10] and Elizabeth Fox-Genovese's assertion that history is present in a text in the form of structure ("Language, practice, and imagination all emerge from history understood as structure, as sets or systems of relations of superordination or subordination"[11]) support the idea that there is always a convergence between the textual and the extratextual in literary representation. The nature of this interaction between fictional texts and external and identifiable realities is what is of concern in the theorizing of representation in minority texts.

Contemporary theory does not envision that art is separate from social reality, that social reality simply predetermines the shape and content of artistic works, or that art alone can successfully refashion social reality. Theory discounts a purely deterministic or mechanistic relationship between art and society and a phenomenological reading of creative activity. Critical and cultural theory, however, accepts the notion that literary works are relatively autonomous, that "their status [is] evidence of the human capacity to respond, and, not merely react, to the social and cultural conditions of the time and place of their production."[12] Literary works, especially minority texts which are infused with references to historical and social realities, continue to perform as acts of imaginative representation and as ideological discourse: "If literary texts are 'functions, or articulations' of their historical contexts, it does not follow that they are nothing but 'records' or 'reflections' of such contexts."[13]

Literary production is perceived to be the result of a series of negotiations "between a creator or a class of creators, equipped with a complex, communally shared repertoire of conventions, and the institutions and practices of society."[14] The fruition of this process of exchange, involving ideological/cultural revisions, technical manipulations, and the constructions and reconstructions of comprehensible realities, envelops the content and form of literary texts. Textual representation participates in the reassembling of social realities and is not, as such, an "objective" delineation of external realities.

Literary representation is about referentiality and this referentiality takes many forms. Stephen Greenblatt states that "literary criticism has a familiar set of terms for the relationship between a work of art and the historical events to which it refers: we speak of allusion, symbolization, allegorization . . . and above all mimesis."[15] In his analysis of Charles Dickens' fiction, Terry Eagleton speaks of formal structures in terms of their correspondence with and allusion to extratextual reality: "The anarchic, decentred, fragmented forms of the early novels correspond in general to an earlier less organised phase of industrial capitalism; the unified structures of the mature fiction allude to a more intensively coordinated capitalism, with its complex networks of finance capitalism."[16] Ideas about correspondence and allusion used to typify the nature of representation in literary texts work against the notion that literature presents an objective depiction of external realities. The conventions of realism, including types of documentation and description, are particular literary modes among a variety of techniques that the writer can utilize in reconstructing lived experience. In the social sciences, even "objective" renderings and analyses of social reality are in themselves individual acts of textual production and are non-literary reconstructions of identifiable events and actions. Pauline Marie Rosenau believes that the rejection of a "positivist, empiricist rational-logical model of modern science"[17] has important implications not just in terms of the methods of analysis, but also in the way that social reality is interpreted. Postmodernists in the social sciences "offer indeterminacy rather than determinism, diversity rather than unity, difference rather than synthesis, complexity rather than simplification."[18]

The questioning of objectivity and authority does not mean that social and cultural analysis is simply relative and therefore unable to come to grips with what actually comprises social reality. Instead this form of analysis affirms that observations and data about social reality frequently are made to fit particular ideological projects. Critiquing postmodernism's refusal to admit to its political positions, Robin Mathews stresses that "philosophic theoreticians are . . . people engaged with real societies and real human life, that they have intentions, and that they live, ultimately, in a moral world in which their choices and the actions that arise out of those choices have effects."[19] Social reality is constructed and maintained by individuals and groups and is not in and of itself self-generating. John Ralston Saul contends that "society functions today largely on the relationship between groups."[20] In identifying various ideologies that help to initiate and sustain group relationships, "we might train ourselves to see the shapes of our reality."[21]

The theorizing of what constitutes the operations of ethnic texts has to pay attention to the interrelatedness between sociology and representation, between social reality and literary activity. Modes of representation, the specific imaginative interpretations of historical and social realities, the revising of cultural ideologies, the repositioning of individual subjectivities, and the recognizing of numerous and contradictory social and ideological forces that influence writers and members of minority groups make up the discursive terrain of minority texts. Ethnic writing involves constant exchanges between these factors that affect the transmission of meaning. By examining the relations between minority texts and the many social/ideological frameworks in which they are positioned, theory can better contextualize the signifying practices of minority literatures.

Addressing the formal structures of fictional work by postcolonial writers, Arun Mukherjee insists on the interrelatedness between text and social reality: "The new Commonwealth novelists, then, have to build structures which allow them to capture the spider-web relationships which constitute community life in the developing countries. These structures may seem loose or episodic to the western critic, yet they have a coherence if judged in accordance with the forms of experience they set out to explore . . . [These writers make] use of parabolic structures, indigenous story telling conventions, folk tales, parodies of western and indigenous forms and rituals."[22]

M. G. Vassanji's novel *No New Land* (1991) develops connections between colonial and family history, the process of immigration and adjustment in Canada, intra-family and intra-community relations and the construction of South Asian Canadian identities. The novel brings together competing ideological and cultural views and intermixes indigenous South Asian forms of storytelling with a realist narrative. This literary text, like other work by South Asian Canadian writers, incorporates, according to Frank Birbalsingh, "subjects, themes, and attitudes that are as much South Asian as Canadian."[23] Similarly, in *Keeper 'N Me* (1994), by Richard Wagamese, conflicting ideas about community, tradition, technology, consumerism, and the role of nature are transmitted through an array of representational techniques, which blend a multi-voiced form of aboriginal storytelling with narrative conventions from mainstream literature. Joseph Pivato maintains that "Italian oral stories about immigrants are the basis for Italian Canadian fiction"[24] and that they demonstrate the relationship between cultural influence and literary representation. He also notes that "regional writers, Rudy Wiebe and Robert Kroetsch, were challenging the conventions of an anglocentric national literature by consciously turning to forgotten forms such as oral narratives from native people, rural folk, the poor, the marginalized."[25] Social relations and representational strategies are inextricably linked together and the correlating of this intra/extratextual system of signification is crucial to the theorizing of minority texts.

"Such writing," states Thomas Ferraro, "challenges the critic to determine how sociological inquiry and literary inventiveness serve one another; where local understandings face off against national constructions of individuality, family, and community; and which strategies of minority-culture self-representation and majority-culture literary forms undergo reciprocal transformations."[26] The choice of literary techniques depends on the ideological complexities of the recreated experiences. There is a coinciding of the functions and effects of particular techniques and of specific social and cultural developments in intra-minority and minority-majority relations.

The citing of the use that irony and juxtaposition are put to in minority literature provides worthwhile examples of the connections between cultural experience and the choice of literary technique. Linda Hutcheon asserts that irony emits contradiction, multiplicity, complicity, marginality, and inclusiveness, and is best suited for dramatizing cultural resistance and heterogeneity. Minorities are faced with a complex set of choices and circumstances in redefining community and cultural identity in the host country: "mapping differences can be a positive as well as a negative thing; it can be a way of celebrating those differences (while still remaining within Canadian culture) and of resisting assimilation."[27] The cultural condition of minority groups of being "paradoxically both marginal and typical"[28] is represented in literary texts through the use of irony. Irony imparts ideas about cultural difference and underlines the ethnic subject's ambivalence both towards established patterns in the ethnic/racial community and new modes of living in mainstream society: "Irony allows 'the other' to address the dominant culture from within the culture's own set of values and modes of understanding, without being co-opted by it and without sacrificing the right to dissent, contradict, and resist."[29]

Juxtaposition, another recurrent formal element in minority literature, is, according to William Boelhower, a crucial component of a semiotic field and a sign-making process that spawn "an open series of binary categories"[30] and help to form the portrayal of ethnicity. The juxtaposing of multiple and contentious cultural frames, through such referents as image clusters, symbolism, and descriptions of specific social and physical environments, thematizes the realities of cultural otherness and the formation of a multifarious subjectivity. In the application of his theoretical position to Italian Canadian writing, William Boelhower argues that minority writing develops a "stereoscopic" perspective as part of the way that "the ethnic subject proceeds in creating ethnic space within Canadian culture."[31] Juxtaposition as an organizing formal device, to a great extent, is a manifestation of the redrawing of cultural lines and the imprinting of a new consciousness: "And the ethnic subject produces difference by thinking differently, that is, by questioning the original project of the immigrant fathers and mothers. In effect, ethnic semiosis as poiesis means recounting a rival story, what we might call a mapping exercise in ethnic tracing, an attempt to recount a series of micro-differences."[32]

The exchanges between cultural context and literary representation clear a space for the presence of human agency. The relative autonomy of texts allows texts "to crystallize the pervasive discourses of any society and thus to shape their development."[33] However, the relative autonomy of texts implies that their ability to affect change "derives precisely from their inscription in a history reread as structured relations"[34] of dominance and subservience. Terry Eagleton sees a dialectical relationship between texts and ideologies — between representations and external belief systems — which does not reduce texts to replicators and promulgators of prevailing sociopolitical orders: "This complex movement [between text and ideology] cannot be imaged as the 'structure of the text' transposing or reproducing the 'structure of ideology': it can only be grasped as a ceaseless reciprocal operation of text on ideology and ideology on text, a mutual structuring and destructuring in which the text constantly overdetermines its own determinations."³⁵ Eagleton is careful to point out that texts are imbricated in a group of identifiable socio-ideological relations and corresponding forms of representation: "Ideology presents itself to the text as a set of significations which are already articulated in a certain form or series of forms . . . Ideology also presents to the text a determinate series of specific modes and mechanisms of aesthetic production — an ideologically determined set of possible modes of aesthetically producing ideological significations."³⁶

Texts as embodiments and constructions of various subject-positions take part in the elucidating and rethinking of social and cultural ideologies. It is in this sense that texts construct subjects and subject-positions which are connected to various ideological discourses that are in circulation in the social order. The identification of subjects with specific ideological discourses is a vital part of textual representation. Ideological discourses provide not only an explanation of reality, but also reinvent ideas about what is assumed to be reality. According to John Mowitt, "the text names the process of cultural construction that both compromises and comprises the subject."³⁷ "Subjectivity is constructed through ideological intervention," Paul Smith surmises, "and that 'subjects' are interpellated, called into position by specific social discourses."³⁸ Since "ideological interpellations" (the signalling of numerous types of ideological positions to the subject) do not "form any kind of unified ideology" (one that is not characterized by gaps and contradictions), then "there seems to be no reason to believe that there exists a correspondingly unified subjectivity."³⁹

The discontinuities and discrepancies in ideological positions and the idea that texts are reinterpreters and producers of ideologies support the notion that texts represent a variety of human agency. Individual and group choices, responses, and attitudes are communicated through subject-positions and mirror the incongruities and disruptions of the surrounding social order. In a text, the subject might appear to be "the effect of a given signifying practice."⁴⁰ Yet the subject is assembled in the text through a process of interpellation that is "various,"⁴¹ and is part of the social system. The subject is represented as being continually formed and reformed by an "almost limitless production of discourses, texts, and addresses which together constitute social life."[42] Human agency is manifested in social life and in texts in terms of challenges and resistance to dominating cultural and social ideologies.

These ideas about ideology, agency, and the textual representation of subject-positions as well as the reimagining of specific cultural ideologies in literary texts set the stage for the theorizing of identity, subject positionality, and culture in minority literature.

One of the tendencies of Subaltern Studies, according to Gayatri Spivak, is that they "rely on certain humanistic notions such as agency, totality, and presence."[43] The valorization of essentialism, the describing of ethnicity as essence and not as a cultural and social construction, functions within a complex political environment. In this environment, an essentialist ethnicity is a means to resist the hegemonic inclinations of the dominant culture. "Wittingly or unwittingly, Subaltern Studies deploys essentialism as a provisional gesture," Diana Fuss maintains, "in order to align themselves with the very subjects who have been written out of conventional historiography."[44] The privileging of an organic and transhistorical cultural experience in the face of potentially exterminating hegemonic forces is not the only political strategy for resistance that is evident in minority discourse.

As part of the cultural production of meanings, ethnicity interrogates widespread constructions of reality by pointing to a discontinuous sociopolitical landscape steeped in competing and overlapping cultural ideologies. The identities of minority subjects are composed of multiple and opposed cultural and socio-ideological positions. Ethnic subjects are comprised by "cultural overdeterminations"[45] from inside minority communities, within the many structures of the dominant society, and as a result of the interactions between ethnic enclaves and components of the mainstream. Ethnicity is situated in numerous and conflicting social and ideological sites. What is constant in this process of change is a signifying practice which remains grounded in a historically-specific cultural context. The elements of the culture of a particular collectivity may become transformed by other influences, since a social group's culture is evolving and revising itself in response to altered circumstances. This does not mean that the culture of an ethnic community simply slips away and is replaced by that of the dominant group.

This non-essentialist reading of ethnicity which examines the complexities, contradictions, and instabilities of cultural development does not put under erasure the historically-specific cultural and ideological context of the ethnic subject. Social and political contingency does not nullify the possibility of human agency. The persistence of ethnicity involves the assuming of viewpoints, however partial, contradictory, and impermanent, and the constant deployment of social and economic strategies. The use of theory in the analysis of ethnic experience helps to locate "the disjunctive, fragmented, displaced agency of those who have suffered the sentence of history — subjugation, domination, diaspora, displacement."[46] Minority texts identify human agency within a dynamic socio-economic environment. Ethnic protagonists are represented as taking part in constructing and reconstructing social reality while their identities are shaped by compelling social and historical forces.

In Sky Lee's novel, *Disappearing Moon Cafe* (1991), the protagonists represent the five generations of a particular Chinese Canadian family, and are influenced by cultural and economic factors in China and Canada. At the same time, they are shown to be participants in the development of family history. The caste system of feudal China, the patriarchal-centred structure of the extended family, the difficulties of immigration and adjustment, the experiences of racism, and the reshaping of gender and social roles in capitalist-technological society are intertwined with the various ways that the characters position themselves in their extended family circle and in their Chinese community, and in their relation to white society. The novel presents "Chinese Canadienness" as multi-positionality, as an array of differing and often conflicting identifications with Chinese and English Canadian culture. Despite the tormented, tragic nature of intra-family relationships, partly the product of racist immigration policies and racist socioeconomic structures, and the subsequent Canadianization of new generations of family members, signalling the dying out of traditional customs and beliefs, the novel does not question the importance and legitimacy of Chinese culture in the new society. *Disappearing Moon Cafe* depicts the dialectical relationship between history, culture, and human action, and exposes the complexities and contradictions of Chinese Canadian experience.

The text, however, is not simply a form of literary sociology, in which narrative strategies are just deployed in order to portray lived experience. The novel reconstructs social relations and offers, from out of a spectrum of possible readings of Chinese Canadian experience, particular interpretations of what constitutes Chineseness in English Canadian society. Sky Lee uses numerous literary techniques which communicate her central concerns and present a particular reading of personal and social reality. Chief among these techniques are juxtaposition, multi-vocality (the narrator invokes the individual voices and perspectives of the major and minor characters), the continual moving between past and present, the fragmentation of chronology, the use of irony, and the use of a self-conscious narrator who is aware that she is recreating reality (she even admits that she cannot fill in the missing gaps of the stories that she is telling). Storytelling becomes a means to transmit and maintain cultural history and patterns, to give meaning to immediate experience, and to endlessly create and recreate one's self-image. The narrator-character perpetually revises her Chinese Canadian identity in the process of telling the life stories of the Wong family members and of her own story as a Canadian of Chinese ancestry.

Canadian minority fictional texts, such as *Disappearing Moon Cafe* and *No New Land*, as well as the Italian Canadian fiction analyzed in this book, demonstrate the interrelatedness between history, culture, and literary representation. The meanings transmitted in minority fiction are contextualized within particular social and cultural settings. The relative autonomy of these texts, manifested in their ability to reconstruct and rethink the nature of lived experience, contests a mechanistic reproduction of reality. Representational strategies not only set up correspondences between the text and documented experience, but they also actively rework the cultural and ideological suppositions underlying that experience.

Human agency is also figured in minority texts through the dramatic enactment of the various subject-positions of the protagonists. These subject-positions oppose, complement, and bypass each other. The multi-positionality of minority literature does not undermine the cultural specificity of the stories being told. It points to the complexities and irresolutions of minority discourse.

Current critical and cultural theory permits an analysis of Canadian minority literature, such as the work of Italian Canadian writers examined in this book. This kind of inquiry considers the cultural terrain, technical operation, and epistemological positioning of minority fictional texts. The application of theory assists the literary/cultural critic in discovering how this literature aesthetically and ideologically undertakes the representation of ethnic subjectivity, and rethinks what is constituted as English Canadian social reality. Equally important, theory configures the imaginary of minority fiction and locates it discursively in contemporary Canadian literature.

10

Notes

ONE

1. Danielle Juteau-Lee and Barbara Roberts, "Ethnicity and Femininity," *Canadian Ethnic Studies* Vol. XIII, 1 (1981): 1.
2. Juteau-Lee and Roberts 15.
3. Linda Hutcheon, Introduction, *Other Solitudes: Canadian Multicultural Fictions*, eds. Linda Hutcheon and Marion Richmond (Toronto: Oxford University Press, 1990) 2.
4. Peter Li, *Ethnic Inequality* (Toronto: Wall and Thompson, 1988) 32.
5. William L. Yancey, Eugene P. Ericksen, and Richard N. Juliani, "Emergent Ethnicity: A Review and Reformulation," *American Sociological Review* Vol. 41, No. 1, (June, 1976) 391.
6. John Edwards, *Language, Society, and Identity* (London, England: Basil Blackwell, 1985) 101.
7. Abdul R. JanMohamed and David Lloyd eds., "Introduction: Toward a Theory of Minority Discourse: What Is to be Done?" *The Nature and Context of Minority Discourse* (New York: Oxford University Press, 1990) 9.
8. Yancey, Ericksen, and Juliani 399.
9. Frank Paci, "Interview by Joseph Pivato," *Other Solitudes: Canadian Multicultural Fictions*, eds. Linda Hutcheon and Marion Richmond (Toronto: Oxford University Press, 1990) 229.
10. Yancey, Erickson, and Juliani 399-400.
11. JanMohamed and Lloyd 4, 15.
12. R. Radhakrishnan, "Ethnic Identity and Post-Structuralist Differance," *The Nature and Context of Minority Discourse*, eds. Abdul R. JanMohamed and David Lloyd (New York: Oxford University Press, 1990) 67.
13. Yancey, Erickson, and Juliani 400.
14. John Zucchi, *Italians in Toronto: Development of a National Identity, 1875-1935* (Kingston and Montreal: McGill-Queen's University Press, 1988) 7.
15. Robert F. Harney, "How to Write a History of Postwar Toronto Italia," *Italians In Ontario*, eds. Franc Sturino and John Zucchi (Toronto: The Multicultural History Society of Ontario, Fall/Winter 1985) 61.
16. Harney, *Italians in Ontario* 61.
17. Giuliana Colalillo, "The Italian Immigrant Family," *Italians in Ontario*, 119.
18. Robert F. Harney, "Italian Immigration and the Frontiers of Western Civilization," *The Italian Immigrant Experience*, eds. John Potestio and

Antonio Pucci (Thunder Bay, Ontario: Canadian Italian Historical Association, 1988) 23.
19. Franc Sturino, "Family and Kin Cohesion Among South Italian Immigrants in Toronto," *The Italian Immigrant Woman in North America*, eds. Betty Boyd Caroli, Robert F. Harney and Lydio F. Tomasi (Toronto: The Multicultural History Society of Ontario, 1978) 291.
20. Roberto Perin, "Introduction: The Immigrant: Actor or Outcast," *Arrangiarsi: The Italian Immigration Experience in Canada*, eds. Roberto Perin and Franc Sturino (Montreal: Guernica Editions, 1989) 18.
21. Perin 18.
22. Perin 25.
23. Perin 21.
24. Leo Cellini, "Emigration, the Italian Family, and Changing Roles," *The Italian Immigrant Woman in North America*, 274.
25. Cellini 281.
26. Edward C. Banfield, *The Moral Basis of a Backward Society* (London, England: The Free Press, 1958) 103.
27. Clifford J. Jansen, *Italians in a Multicultural Canada* (Queenston, Ontario: The Edwin Mellen Press, 1988) 83.
28. Franc Sturino, "Family and Kin Cohesion Among South Italian Immigrants in Toronto," *The Italian Immigrant Woman in North America*, 293.
29. Colleen L. Johnson, "The Maternal Role in the Contemporary Italian American Family," *The Italian Immigrant Woman in North America*, 237.
30. Humbert S. Nelli, *From Immigrants to Ethnics: The Italian Americans* (New York: Oxford University Press, 1983) 133.
31. Johnson 234.
32. Franca Iacovetta, "From Contadina to Worker: Southern Italian Working Women in Toronto, 1947-1962," *Italians in Ontario*, 93.
33. Johnson 240.
34. Iacovetta 91.
35. Iacovetta 92.
36. Bruno Ramirez, *The Italians in Canada* (Canadian Historical Society, 1990) 14.
37. Nelli 137.
38. Nelli 137.
39. Ramirez 14.
40. Franc Sturino, *The Italian Immigrant Woman in North America*, 299.
41. Sturino 300.
42. William Boelhower, *Through a Glass Darkly: Ethnic Semiosis in American Literature* (Venezia: Edizioni Helvetia, 1984) 27.
43. Boelhower 104.
44. Boelhower 120.
45. Boelhower 135.
46. Sneja Gunew, "Forward: Speaking to Joseph," *Echo: Essays on Other Literatures* by Joseph Pivato (Toronto: Guernica Editions, 1994) 21.

47. Myrna Kostash, "Pens of Many Colours," *The Canadian Forum* Vol. LXVIV No. 790 (June, 1990) 17-18.
48. Antonio D'Alfonso, "The Road Between: Essentialism. For an Italian Culture in Quebec and Canada," *Contrasts: Comparative Essays on Italian-Canadian Writing*, ed. Joseph Pivato (Montreal: Guernica Editions, 1985) 211.
49. Frank Paci, "An Interview with Frank G. Paci by C.D. Minni," *Canadian Literature* No. 16 (Fall, 1985) 12.
50. D'Alfonso 211.
51. D'Alfonso 212.
52. D'Alfonso 226.
53. William Boelhower, "Italo-Canadian Poetry and Ethnic Semiosis in the Postmodern Context,"*Arrangiarsi: The Italian Immigration Experience in Canada*, eds. Roberto Perin and Franc Sturino (Montreal: Guernica Editions, 1989) 232-233.
54. Boelhower 231.
55. Boelhower 232.
56. Eli Mandel, "The Ethnic Voice in Canadian Writing," *Figures in a Ground: Canadian Essays On Modern Literature*, eds. Diane Bessai and David Jackel (Saskatoon: Western Producer Books, 1978) 274.
57. Mary Jo Bona ed., Introduction, *The Voices We Carry: Recent Italian/American Women's Fiction* (Montreal: Guernica Editions, 1994) 23.
58. Helen Barolini ed., Introduction, *The Dream Book: An Anthology of Writings by Italian American Women* (New York: Schocken Books, 1985) xiii.
59. Linda Hutcheon, *Splitting Images: Contemporary Canadian Ironies* (Toronto: Oxford University Press, 1991) 48.
60. Hutcheon, *Splitting Images* 53.
61. Bruce Elder, "Desperately Seeking Irony in Canada," *The Literary Review of Canada* Vol. 1, No. 5 (May, 1992) 5.
62. Joseph Pivato, "A Literature of Exiles: Italian Language Writing in Canada," *Contrasts: Comparative Essays on Italian-Canadian Writing*, 175.
63. Alexandre L. Amprimoz and Sante A. Viselli, "Death Between Two Cultures: Italian-Canadian Poetry," *Contrasts: Comparative Essays on Italian-Canadian Writing* 104.
64. Boelhower, *Arrangiarsi* 231.
65. Linda Hutcheon, *Other Solitudes: Canadian Multicultural Fictions* 12.
66. Thomas J. Ferraro, *Ethnic Passages: Literary Immigrants in Twentieth-Century America* (Chicago: The University of Chicago Press, 1993) 21.
67. Ferraro 72.
68. Hutcheon, *Splitting Images: Contemporary Canadian Ironies* 52.
69. Tamara J. Palmer, "The Fictionalization of the Vertical Mosaic: The Immigrant, Success, and National Mythology," *Literatures of Lesser Diffusion*, ed. Joseph Pivato (Edmonton: Research Institute of Comparative Studies, 1990) 75, 101.
70. Ferraro 10.
71. Palmer 69-70.

Notes

72. Nino Ricci, "Recreating Paradise: An Interview with Nino Ricci by Jeffrey Canton," *Paragraph* Vol. 13, No. 3 (1991) 4.
73. Francesco Loriggio, "History, Literary History, and Ethnic Literature," *Literatures of Lesser Diffusion*, 30.
74. Loriggio 41.
75. Loriggio 34.
76. Joseph Pivato, "Italian-Canadian Women Writers Recall History," *Canadian Ethnic Studies* Vol. XVIII, No. 1 (1986) 80.
77. Pivato, *Canadian Ethnic Studies* 80.
78. R. Radhakrishnan, *The Nature and Context of Minority Discourse* 62.
79. Loriggio 42.
80. Loriggio 25.
81. Wolfgang Karrer and Hartmut Lutz eds., "Minority Literatures in North America: From Cultural Nationalism to Liminality," *Minority Literatures in North America: Contemporary Perspectives* (New York: Peter Lang, 1990) 35.
82. Loriggio 34.

TWO

1. Frank Paci, "Tasks of the Canadian Novelist on Immigrant Themes," *Contrasts: Comparative Essays on Italian-Canadian Writing*, ed. Joseph Pivato (Montreal: Guernica Editions, 1985) 54.
2. Linda Hutcheon, *Splitting Images: Contemporary Canadian Ironies* (Toronto: Oxford University Press, 1991) 52.
3. Eli Mandel, Introduction, *Under the Ribs of Death* by John Marlyn (Toronto: McClelland and Stewart, 1971) 11.
4. Hutcheon, *Splitting Images: Contemporary Canadian Ironies* 57.
5. Hutcheon, *Splitting Images* 56-57.
6. Linda Hutcheon, "'A Lightness of Thoughtfulness': The Power of Postmodern Irony," *Open Letter* 8, No. 1 (1991) 69.
7. Hutcheon, *Open Letter* 69, 70.
8. Hutcheon, *Splitting Images* 52.
9. Frank Paci, *Black Madonna* (Ottawa: Oberon Press, 1982) 53. (Further references will be in the text.)
10. Frank Paci, *Contrasts: Comparative Essays on Italian-Canadian Writing* 57.
11. Paci, *Contrasts: Comparative Essays on Italian-Canadian Writing* 57.
12. Roberta Sciff-Zamaro, "*Black Madonna:* A Search for the Great Mother," *Contrasts: Comparative Essays on Italian-Canadian Writing* 90, 87, 89.
13. Sciff-Zamaro 90.
14. Julie Beddoes, "Sandor, Alex and the rest: multiplication of the subject in John Marlyn's *Under the Ribs of Death*," *Open Letter* 6, No. 8 (1985) 7-8.
15. Hutcheon, *Splitting Images: Contemporary Canadian Ironies* 52.
16. Martin Waxman, "Profile/Frank Paci: The Discipline of Discovery," *Books in Canada* (November, 1994) 22.

THREE

1. C. D. Minni, "The Short Story as an Ethnic Genre," *Contrasts: Comparative Essays on Italian-Canadian Writing*, ed. Joseph Pivato (Montreal: Guernica Editions, 1985) 74.
2. Wolfgang Karrer and Hartmut Lutz eds., "Minority Literatures in North America: From Cultural Nationalism to Liminality," *Minority Literatures in North America: Contemporary Perspectives* (New York: Peter Lang, 1990) 49-50.
3. Minni, *Contrasts: Comparative Essays on Italian-Canadian Writing* 65, 69.
4. William Boelhower, "Italo-Canadian Poetry and Ethnic Semiosis in the Postmodern Context," *Arrangiarsi: The Italian Immigration Experience in Canada*, eds. Roberto Perin and Franc Sturino (Montreal: Guernica Editions, 1989) 235, 240.
5. Karrer and Lutz 34-35.
6. C. D. Minni, *Other Selves* (Montreal: Guernica Editions, 1985) 35. (Further references will be in the text.)
7. Linda Hutcheon, *Splitting Images: Contemporary Canadian Ironies* (Toronto: Oxford University Press, 1991) 55.
8. William Boelhower, *Through a Glass Darkly: Ethnic Semiosis in American Literature* (Venezia: Edizione Helveta, 1984) 88.
9. Karrer and Lutz 26.
10. Minni, *Contrasts: Comparative Essays on Italian-Canadian Writing* 68.
11. Boelhower, *Arrangiarsi: The Italian Immigration Experience in Canada* 233.
12. Boelhower, *Through a Glass Darkly: Ethnic Semiosis in American Literature* 135.
13. C. D Minni, "Changes," *Ricordi: Things Remembered: An Anthology of Short Stories*, ed. C. D. Minni (Montreal: Guernica Editions, 1989) 180. (Further references will be in the text.)
14. Hutcheon 60.
15. Roberta Sciff-Zamaro, rev. of *Other Selves*, by C.D. Minni, *Canadian Ethnic Studies* Vol. XVII, No. 3 1986: 155.
16. Boelhower, *Through a Glass Darkly: Ethnic Semiosis in American Literature* 131.
17. Karrer and Lutz 25.
18. Boelhower, *Arrangiarsi: The Italian Immigration Experience* 241.

FOUR

1. Nino Ricci, *Lives of the Saints* (Dunvegan, Ontario: Cormorant Books, 1990) 131. (Further references will be in the text.)
2. Francesco Loriggio, "The Question of Corpus: Ethnicity and Canadian Literature," *Future Indicative: Literary Theory and Canadian Literature*, ed. John Moss (Ottawa: University of Ottawa Press, 1987) 61.
3. Loriggio, *Future Indicative: Literary Theory and Canadian Literature* 61.

4. Loriggio, *Future Indicative: Literary Theory and Canadian Literature* 63, 60.
5. Nino Ricci, "Recreating Paradise: An Interview with Nino Ricci by Jeffrey Canton," *Paragraph* Vol. 13, No. 13 (1991): 6.
6. Ricci, *Paragraph* 5.
7. Francesco Loriggio, "Italian-Canadian Literature: Basic Critical Issues," *Writers in Transition: The Proceedings of the First Annual Conference of Italian-Canadian Writers*, eds. C. Dino Minni and Anna Foschi Ciampolini (Montreal: Guernica Editions, 1990) 92.
8. Ricci, *Paragraph* 4.
9. Ricci, *Paragraph* 5.
10. Stephen Slemon, "Magic Realism: A Post-Colonial Discourse," *Canadian Literature* No. 116 (Spring/1988) 17.
11. Slemon 16.
12. Ricci, *Paragraph* 5.

FIVE

1. Franca Iacovetta, "Trying to Make Ends Meet: An Historical Look at Italian Immigrant Women, the State and Family Survival Strategies in Post-War Toronto," *Canadian Women Studies* Vol. 8, No. 2 (Summer, 1987) 10.
2. Iacovetta 6.
3. Helen Barolini, Preface, *The Dream Book: An Anthology of Writings by Italian American Women* (New York: Shocken Books, 1985) 13.
4. Barolini xiv.
5. Enoch Padolsky, "Establishing the Two-Way Street: Literary Criticism and Ethnic Studies," *Canadian Ethnic Studies* XXII, 1 (1990) 32.
6. Maria J. Ardizzi, Preface, *Made In Italy*, trans. Anna Maria Castrilli (Toronto: Toma Publishing Inc., 1982) xi. (Further references will be in the text.)
7. Alexandre L. Amprimoz and Sante A. Viselli, "Death Between Two Cultures: Italian-Canadian Poetry," *Contrasts: Comparative Essays on Italian-Canadian Writing*, ed. Joseph Pivato (Montreal: Guernica Editions, 1985) 113.
8. Antonino Mazza, Introduction, *The Way I Remember It* (Montreal: Guernica Editions, 1992) 11.
9. Amprimoz and Viselli 118.
10. Amprimoz and Viselli 108.
11. Tamara J. Palmer, "The Fictionalization of the Vertical Mosaic: The Immigrant, Success, and National Mythology," *Literatures of Lesser Diffusion*, ed. Joseph Pivato (Edmonton: Research Institute of Comparative Studies, 1990) 83.
12. Enoch Padolsky 10.
13. John Roberts, "Irony in an Immigrant Novel: John Marlyn's *Under the Ribs of Death*," *Canadian Ethnic Studies* XIV, 1 (1982) 41.
14. Beverly Rasporich, "Retelling Vera Lysenko: A Feminist and Ethnic Writer," *Canadian Ethnic Studies* XXI, 2 (1989) 41.

15. Rasporich 49-50.
16. Barolini 35-36.

SIX

1. Robert Kroetsch, "The Grammar of Silence," *The Lovely Treachery of Words: Essays Selected and New* (Toronto: Oxford University Press, 1989) 89.
2. Caterina Edwards, *The Lion's Mouth* (Edmonton: NeWest, 1982) 10. Reprinted by Guernica Editions, 1993. (Further references will be in the NeWest edition.)
3. Francesco Loriggio, "History, Literary History, and Ethnic Literature," *Literatures of Lesser Diffusion*, ed. Joseph Pivato (Edmonton: Research Institute of Comparative Studies, 1990) 35.
4. Arnold Itwaru, *The Invention of Canada: Literary Text and the Immigrant Imaginary* (Toronto: Tsar, 1990) 19.
5. Mikhail Bakhtin, *Rabelais and His World*, trans. Helene Iswolsky (Cambridge, Mass. and London, England: MIT Press, 1965) 10.
6. Helen Barolini, Introduction, *The Dream Book: An Anthology of Writings by Italian American Women* (New York: Shocken Books, 1985) 11.
7. Joseph Pivato, "Italian-Canadian Women Writers Recall History," *Canadian Ethnic Studies* XVIII, 1, (1986) 83.

SEVEN

1. Darlene Madott, *Bottled Roses* (Ottawa: Oberon Press, 1985) 9. (Further references will be in the text.)
2. Linda Hutcheon, *Splitting Images: Contemporary Canadian Ironies* (Toronto: Oxford University Press, 1991) 99.
3. Helen Barolini, Introduction, *The Dream Book: An Anthology of Writings by Italian American Women* (New York: Shocken Books, 1985) 9.
4. Pia Pichini, "Two Generations in Conflict: Sex Role Expectations Among Italian-Canadian Women," *Canadian Women Studies* Vol. 8, Number 2 (Summer, 1987) 22.
5. Genni Donati Gunn, "Avoiding the Stereotypes," *Writers In Transition: The Proceedings of the First Annual Conference of Italian-Canadian Writers*, (Montreal: Guernica Press, 1990) 142.
6. Gunn 143.

EIGHT

1. Homi Bhabha, *Nation and Narration* (London: Routledge, 1990) 313.
2. Bhabha 317.
3. Bhabha 317.
4. Sneja Ganew, "Feminism/Theory/Postcolonialism: Agency Without Identity," Conference Paper, Edmonton, Sept. 16, 1992: 18.
5. Lucy R. Lippard, *Mixed Blessings: New Art in a Multicultural America* (New York: Pantheon Books, 1990) 156.

Notes

6. Linda Hutcheon, *Splitting Images: Contemporary Canadian Ironies* (Toronto: Oxford University Press, 1991) 51.
7. William Boelhower, "Italo-Canadian Poetry And Ethnic Semiosis," *Arrangiarsi: The Italian Immigration Experience in Canada*, eds. Roberto Perin and Franc Sturino (Montreal: Guernica Editions, 1992) 237.
8. Antonino Mazza, Introduction, *The Way I Remember It* (Guernica Editions: Montreal, 1992) 12-13.
9. Mazza 52.

NINE

1. Aram H. Veeser, Introduction, *The New Historicism*. ed. H. Aram Veeser. (New York: Routledge, 1989) xi.
2. Veeser xiii.
3. Terry Eagleton, *Criticism and Ideology: A Study in Marxist Literary Theory* (London: Verso, 1985) 72.
4. Elizabeth Fox-Genovese, "Literary Criticism and the Politics of the New Historicism," *The New Historicism* (New York: Routledge, 1989) 221.
5. Janet Wolff, *The Social Production Of Art* (New York: New York University Press, 1981) 2.
6. Arnold Itwaru, *The Invention of Canada: Literary Text and the Immigrant Imaginary* (Toronto: TSAR Publications, 1990) 26.
7. Arnold Itwaru 25.
8. Robin Mathews, *The Treason of The Intellectuals: English Canada in the Post-Modern Period* (Prescott, Ontario: Voyageur Publishing, 1995) 40.
9. James Laxer, *False God* (Toronto: Lester Publishing Limited, 1993) 2.
10. Terry Eagleton 72.
11. Elizabeth Fox-Genovese 221.
12. Hayden White, "New Historicism: A Comment," *The New Historicism*. (New York: Routledge, 1989) 299.
13. Hayden White, 299.
14. Stephen Greenblatt, "Towards a Poetics of Culture," *The New Historicism* (New York: Routledge, 1989) 12.
15. Stephen Greenblatt 11.
16. Terry Eagleton 130.
17. Pauline Marie Rosenau, *Post-Modernism And The Social Sciences: Insights, Inroads, And Intrusions* (Princeton, New Jersey: Princeton University Press, 1992) 9.
18. Pauline Marie Rosenau 8.
19. Robin Mathews 22.
20. John Ralston Saul, *The Unconscious Civilization* (Concord, Ontario: House of Anansi Press Limited, 1995) 31.
21. John Ralston Saul 29.
22. Arun Mukherjee, *Towards an Aesthetic of Opposition: Essays on Literature, Criticism and Cultural Imperialism* (Stratford, Ontario: Williams-Wallace Publishers, 1988) 17.

23. Frank Birbalsingh, "South Asian Canadian Novels in English," *A Meeting of Streams: South Asian Canadian Literature*. ed. M. G. Vassanji (Toronto: TSAR Publications, 1985) 60.
24. Joseph Pivato, *Echo: Essays on Other Literatures* (Toronto: Guernica Editions, 1994) 81.
25. Joseph Pivato 80.
26. Thomas J. Ferraro, *Ethnic Passages: Literary Immigrants in Twentieth-Century America* (Chicago: The University of Chicago Press, 1993) 3.
27. Linda Hutcheon, "'The Canadian Mosaic: A Melting Pot on Ice': The Ironies of Ethnicity and Race," *Splitting Images: Contemporary Canadian Ironies* (Toronto: Oxford University Press, 1991) 52.
28. Linda Hutcheon 52.
29. Linda Hutcheon 49.
30. William Boelhower, "Italo-Canadian Poetry and Ethnic Semiosis in the Postmodern Context," *Arrangarsi: The Italian Immigration Experience in Canada*. ed. Roberto Perin and Franc Sturino (Montreal: Guernica Editions, 1992) 231.
31. William Boelhowver 231.
32. William Boelhowever 237.
33. Elizabeth Fox-Genovese 222.
34. Elizabeth Fox-Genovese 222.
35. Terry Eagleton 99.
36. Terry Eagleton 100.
37. John Mowitt, Forward, *Discerning the Subject* (Minneapolis, Minnesota: University of Minnesota Press, 1988) xix.
38. Paul Smith, *Discerning the Subject* (Minneapolis, Minnesota: University of Minnesota Press, 1988) 17.
39. Paul Smith 18.
40. Paul Smith 31.
41. Paul Smith 31.
42. Paul Smith 31.
43. Diana Fuss, *Essentially Speaking: Feminism, Nature, and Difference* (New York: Routledge, 1989) 31.
44. Diana Fuss 31.
45. Diana Fuss 75.
46. Homi K. Bhabha, "Postcolonial Authority and Postmodern Guilt," *Cultural Studies*. eds. Lawrence Grossberg, Cary Nelson, and Paula Treichler (New York: Routledge, 1992) 56.

11
List of Works Cited

Primary Texts

Ardizzi, Maria J. *Made in Italy*. Toronto: Toma Publishing Inc., 1982.
Edwards, Caterina. *The Lion's Mouth*. Edmonton: NeWest, 1982. Reprinted by Guernica Editions, 1993.
Madott, Darlene. *Bottled Roses*. Ottawa: Oberon Press, 1985.
Minni, C.D. Minni. *Other Selves*. Montreal, Guernica Editions, 1985.
Minni, C.D. Minni. "Changes." *Ricordi: Things Remembered: An Anthology of Short Stories*. Ed. C.D. Minni. Montreal: Guernica Editions, 1989. 171-184.
Paci, Frank. *Black Madonna*. Ottawa: Oberon Press, 1982.
Ricci, Nino. *Lives of the Saints*. Dunvegan, Ontario: Cormorant Books, 1990.

Secondary Texts

Books

Amprimoz, Alexander L. and Viselli, Sante A. "Death Between Two Cultures: Italian-Canadian Poetry." *Contrasts: Comparative Essays on Italian-Canadian Writing*. Ed. Joseph Pivato. Montreal: Guernica Editions, 1985.
Bakhtin, Mikhail. *Rabelais and His World*, trans. Helene Iswolsky. Cambridge, Mass. and London, England: MIT Press, 1965.
Banfield, Edward. *The Moral Basis of a Backward Society*. London, England: The Free Press, 1958.
Barolini, Helen. Introduction. *The Dream Book: An Anthology of Writings by Italian American Women*. Ed. Helen Barolini. New York: Schoken Books, 1985.
Bhabha, Homi. *Nation and Narration*. London: Routledge, 1990.
———. "Postcolonial Authority and Postmodern Guilt." *Cultural Studies*. Ed. Lawrence Grossberg, Cary Nelson, and Paula Treichler. New York: Routledge, 1992.
Birbalsingh, Frank. "South Asian Canadian Novels in English." *A Meeting of Streams: South Asian Canadian Literature*. Ed. M. G. Vassanji. Toronto: TSAR Publications, 1985.
Boelhower, William. *Through a Glass Darkly: Ethnic Semiosis in American Literature*. Venezia: Edizioni Helvetia, 1984.
———. "Italo-Canadian Poetry and Ethnic Semiosis in the Postmodern Context." *Arrangiarsi: The Italian Immigrant Experience in Canada*.

Ed. Roberto Perin and Franc Sturino. Montreal: Guernica Editions, 1989.

Bona, Mary Jo. Introduction. *The Voices We Carry: Recent Italian/American Women's Fiction*. Ed. Mary Jo Bona. Montreal: Guernica Editions, 1994.

Cellini, Leo. "Emigration, the Italian Family, and Changing Roles." *The Italian Immigrant Woman in North America*. Ed. Betty Boyd Caroli, Robert F. Harney and Lydio F. Tomasi. Toronto: The Multicultural History Society of Ontario, 1978.

Colalillo, Giuliana. "The Italian Immigrant Family." *Italians in Ontario*. Ed. Franc Sturino and John Zucchi. Toronto: The Multicultural History Society of Ontario, Fall/Winter, 1985.

D'Alfonso, Antonio. "The Road Between: Essentialism. For an Italian Culture in Quebec and Canada." Pivato, *Contrasts: Comparative Essays on Italian-Canadian Writing*.

Eagleton, Terry. *Criticism and Ideology: A Study in Marxist Literary Theory*. London: Verso, 1985.

Edwards, John. *Language, Society, and Identity*. London, England: Basil Blackwell, 1985.

Ferraro, Thomas J. *Ethnic Passages: Literary Immigrants in Twentieth-Century America*. Chicago: The University of Chicago Press, 1993.

Fox-Genovese, Elizabeth. "Literary Criticism and the Politics of the New Historicism." *The New Historicism*. New York: Routledge, 1989.

Fuss, Diana. *Essentially Speaking: Feminism, Nature, and Difference*. New York: Routledge, 1989.

Greenblatt, Stephen. "Towards a Poetics of Culture." *The New Historicism*. New York: Routledge, 1989.

Gunew, Sneja. "Forward: Speaking to Joseph." *Echo: Essays on Other Literatures* by Joseph Pivato. Toronto: Guernica Editions, 1994.

Gunn, Genni Donato. "Avoiding the Stereotypes." *Writers in Transition: The Proceedings of the First National Conference of Italian-Canadian Writers*. Ed. C. Dino Minni and Anna Foschi Ciampolini. Montreal: Guernica Editions, 1990.

Harney, Robert F. "How to Write a History of Postwar Toronto Italia." Sturino, *Italians in Ontario*, 1985.

———. "Italian Immigration and the Frontiers of Western Civilization." *The Italian Immigrant Experience*. Ed. John Potesto and Antonio Pucci. Thunder Bay, Ontario: Canadian Historical Association, 1983.

Hutcheon, Linda. Introduction. *Other Solitudes: Canadian Multicultural Fictions*. Ed. Linda Hutcheon and Mary Richmond. Toronto: Oxford University Press, 1990.

———. *Splitting Images: Contemporary Canadian Ironies*. Toronto: Oxford University Press, 1991.

Iacovetta, Franca. "From Contadina to Worker: Southern Italian Working Women in Toronto, 1947-1962." Sturino, *Italians in Ontario*.

Itwaru, Arnold. *The Invention of Canada: Literary Text and the Immigrant Imaginary*. Toronto: TSAR Publications, 1990.

List of Works Cited

JanMohamed, Abdul R. and Lloyd, David, eds. "Introduction: Toward a Theory of Minority Discourse: What Is To Be Done?" *The Nature and Context of Minority Discourse.* New York: Oxford University Press, 1990.

Jansen, Clifford. *Italians in a Multicultural Canada.* Queenston, Ontario: The Edwin Mellen Press, 1988.

Johnson, Colleen L. "The Maternal Role in the Contemporary Italian American Family." Caroli, Harney, and Tomasi, *The Italian Immigrant Woman in North America,* 1978.

Karrer, Wolfgang and Lutz, Hartmut, eds. "Minority Literatures in North America: From Cultural Nationalism to Liminality." *Minority Literatures in North America: Contemporary Perspectives.* New York: Peter Lang, 1990.

Kroetsch, Robert. "The Grammar of Silence." *The Lovely Treachery of Words: Essays Selected and New.* Toronto: Oxford University Press, 1989.

Laxer, James. *False God: How The Globalization Myth Has Impoverished Canada.* Toronto: Lester Publishing Limited, 1993.

Li, Peter. *Ethnic Inequality.* Toronto: Wall and Thompson, 1988.

Lee, Sky. *Disappearing Moon Cafe.* Vancouver: Douglas & McIntyre, 1991.

Lippard, Lucy R. *Mixed Blessings: New Art in a Multicultural America.* New York: Pantheon Books, 1990.

Loriggio, Francesco. "History, Literary History, and Ethnic Literature." *Literatures of Lesser Diffusion.* Ed. Joseph Pivato. Edmonton: Research Institute of Comparative Studies, 1990.

————. "The Question of Corpus: Ethnicity and Canadian Literature." *Future Indicative: Literary Theory and Canadian Literature.* Ed. John Moss. Ottawa: University of Ottawa Press, 1987.

————. "Italian-Canadian Literature: Basic Critical Issues." Minni and Ciampolini, *Writers in Transition: The Proceedings of the First National Conference of Italian-Canadian Writers.*

Mandel, Eli. "The Ethnic Voice in Canadian Writing." *Figures in a Ground: Canadian Essays On Modern Literature.* Ed. Diane Bessai and David Jackel. Saskatoon: Western Producer Books, 1978.

————. "Introduction." *Under the Ribs of Death* by John Marlyn. Toronto: McClelland and Stewart, 1971.

Mathews, Robin. *The Treason of The Intellectuals: English Canada in the Post-Modern Period.* Prescott, Ontario: Voyageur Publishing, 1995.

Mazza, Antonino. Introduction. *The Way I Remember It.* Montreal: Guernica Editions, 1992.

————. "Country, Culture and Context: Re-inventing the Canadian Poetic Voice." *The Way I Remember It.*

Mowitt, John. "Forward." *Discerning the Subject.* Minneapolis, Minnesota: University of Minnesota Press, 1988.

Minni, C.D. "The Short Story as an Ethnic Genre." Pivato, *Contrasts: Comparative Essays on Italian-Canadian Writing.*

Mukherjee, Arun. *Towards an Aesthetic of Opposition: Essays on Literature, Criticism and Cultural Imperialism*. Stratford, Ontario: Williams-Wallace Publishers, 1988.

Nelli, Humbert S. *From Immigrants to Ethnics: The Italian Americans*. New York: Oxford University Press, 1983.

Paci, Frank. "Interview by Joseph Pivato." Hutcheon and Richmond, *Other Solitudes: Canadian Multicultural Fictions*.

——————."Tasks of the Canadian Novelist on Immigrant Themes." *Contrasts: Comparative Essays on Italian-Canadian Writing*.

Palmer, Tamara J. "The Fictionalization of the Vertical Mosaic: The Immigrant, Success, and National Mythology." Pivato, *Literatures of Lesser Diffusion*.

Perin, Roberto. "Introduction: The Immigrant: Actor or Outcast." Perin and Sturino, *Arrangiarsi: The Italian Immigrant Experience in Canada*.

Pivato, Joseph, ed. "A Literature of Exiles: Italian Language Writing in Canada." *Contrasts: Comparative Essays on Italian-Canadian Writing*.

——————. *Echo: Essays on Other Literatures*. Toronto: Guernica Editions, 1994.

Radhakrishnan, R. "Ethnic Identity and Post-Structuralist Difference." JanMohamed and Lloyd, *The Nature and Context of Minority Discourse*, 1990.

Ramirez, Bruno. *The Italians in Canada*. Canadian Historical Society, 1990.

Rosenau, Pauline Marie. *Post-Modernism and the Social Sciences: Insights, Inroads, And Intrusions*. Princeton, New Jersey: Princeton University Press, 1992.

Saul, John Ralston. *The Unconscious Civilization*. Concord, Ontario: House of Anansi Press Limited, 1995.

Sciff-Zamaro, Roberta. "Black Madonna: A Search for the Great Mother." Pivato, *Contrasts: Comparative Essays on Italian-Canadian Writing*.

Smith, Paul. *Discerning the Subject*. Minneapolis, Minnesota: University of Minnesota Press, 1988.

Sturino, Franc. "Family and Kin Cohesion Among South Italian Immigrants in Toronto." Caroli, Harney, and Tomasi, *The Italian Immigrant Woman in North America*, 1978.

Wagamese, Richard. *Keeper'N Me*. Toronto: Doubleday Canada Limited, 1994.

White, Hayden. "New Historicism: A Comment." *The New Historicism*. New York: Routledge, 1989.

Wolff, Janet. *The Social Production of Art*. New York: New York University Press, 1981.

Vassanji, M. G. *No New Land*. Toronto: McClelland And Stewart, 1991.

Veeser, H. Aram. Introduction. *The New Historicism*. Ed. H. Aram Veeser. New York: Routledge, 1989.

Zucchi, John. *Italians in Toronto: Development of a National Identity, 1875-1935*. Kingston and Montreal: McGill-Queen's University Press, 1988.

Articles and Interviews

Beddoes, Julie. "Sandor, Alex and the Rest: Multiplication of the subject in John Marlyn's *Under the Ribs of Death*." *Open Letter.* 6, No. 8 (1985).

Elder, Bruce. "Desperately Seeking Irony in Canada." *The Literary Review of Canada.* Vol. 1, No. 5 (1992).

Gunew, Sneja. "Feminism/Theory/Postcolonialism: Agency Without Identity." A Conference Paper presented in Edmonton (Sept 16, 1992).

Hutcheon, Linda. "'A Lightness of Thoughtfulness': The Power of Postmodern Irony." *Open Letter.* 8, No. 1 (1991).

Iacovetta, Franca. "Trying To Make Ends Meet: An Historical Look at Italian Immigrant Women, the State and Family Survival Strategies in Post-War Toronto." *Canadian Women Studies.* Vol. 8, No. 2 (Summer, 1987).

Kostash, Myrna. "Pens of Many Colours." *The Canadian Forum.* Vol. LXVIV, No. 790 (June, 1990).

Lee-Juteau, Danielle and Roberts, Barbara. "Ethnicity and Femininity." *Canadian Ethnic Studies.* Vol. XIII, No. 1 (1981).

Paci, Frank. "An Interview with Frank G. Paci by C.D. Minni." *Canadian Literature.* No.16 (Fall 1985).

Padolsky, Enoch. "Establishing the Two-Way Street: Literary Criticism and Ethnic Studies." *Canadian Ethnic Studies.* Vol. XXII, No. 1 (1990).

Pivato, Jospeh. "Italian-Canadian Women Writers Recall History." *Canadian Ethnic Studies.* Vol. XVIII, No. 1 (1986).

Pichini, Pia. "Two Generations in Conflict: Sex Role Expectations Among Italian-Canadian Women." *Canadian Women Studies.* Vol. 8, No. 2 (Summer, 1987).

Rasporich, Beverly. "Retelling Vera Lysenko: A Feminist and Ethnic Writer." *Canadian Ethnic Studies.* Vol. XXI, No. 2 (1989).

Ricci, Nino. "Recreating Paradise: An Interview with Nino Ricci by Jeffrey Canton." *Paragraph.* Vol. 13, No. 3 (1991).

Roberts, John. "Irony in an Immigrant Novel: John Marlyn's *Under the Ribs of Death*." *Canadian Ethnic Studies.* Vol. XIV, No. 1 (1982).

Sciff-Zamaro, Roberta. Book Review: *Other Selves. Canadian Ethnic Studies.* Vol. XVII, No. 3 (1986).

Slemon, Stephen. "Magic Realism: A Post-Colonial Discourse." *Canadian Literature.* No. 116 (Spring, 1988).

Waxman, Martin. "Profile/Frank Paci: The Discipline of Discovery." *Books in Canada.* (November, 1994).

Yancey, William L., Ericksen, Eugene P., and Juliani, Richard N. "Emergent Ethnicity: A Review and Reformulation." *American Sociological Review.* Vol. 41, No. 1 (1976).